CHAINS & CASE FILES

Documented Crimes Against the Human Body from Slavery Courts to Modern Records

Azrael Sidiiq

Afrodescendant Solutions

CONTENT ADVISORY NOTICE

This book addresses historical systems of exploitation, coercion, racial violence, and institutional abuse documented in court records, maritime logs, legislative archives, medical journals, and public reports.

Readers will encounter discussion of:

sexual coercion and assault

forced reproduction practices

trafficking and involuntary confinement

lynching and public terror

medical experimentation

economic exploitation of human bodies

psychological domination

and forms of systemic abuse recorded in the language of their time

While this work does not present graphic description, the subject matter reflects documented historical realities that may be disturbing. Reader discretion is advised.

The material is presented for educational, legal, and historical analysis.

Contents

"The past is never dead. It's not even past."

— William Faulkner

"Power concedes nothing without a demand. It never did and it never will."

— Frederick Douglass

"What is written remains."

— Ancient legal maxim

Prologue

PROLOGUE

The Room Where the Files Were Kept

Imagine a room with no windows.

Not abandoned.

Not forgotten.

Preserved.

Shelves rise from floor to ceiling, heavy with boxes that have not been opened in decades, some for centuries. Their labels are handwritten. Their corners are worn. Dust settles on them like time made visible.

Inside those boxes are papers.

Not stories.

Not theories.

Records.

Bills of sale.

Court rulings.

Insurance claims.

Shipping manifests.

Affidavits.

Property inventories.

Each page is calm. Orderly. Administrative. Official.

Nothing about them appears emotional. Nothing about them appears dramatic. They do not shout, accuse, or plead. They simply state facts in the language of bureaucracy.

That is what makes them terrifying.

Because cruelty written as procedure is harder to recognize than cruelty written as violence.

Most people imagine history's worst acts as chaotic explosions of brutality. But the archives show something different: they were often quiet, organized, documented, stamped, and filed.

The world remembers screams.

It rarely remembers paperwork.

This book opens the boxes.

Not to speculate.

To read.

Preface

SCHOLARLY PREFACE

On Method, Documentation, and Ethical Representation

This book is constructed from primary documentation.

Its foundation rests upon:

maritime insurance litigation

probate inventories

plantation ledgers

medical publications

legislative statutes

criminal case files

newspaper archives

commission reports

and institutional memoranda

The decision to write a general-audience edition required restraint. The archival record contains explicit descriptions of sexual violence, mutilation, coercion, humiliation, and systemic degradation. Those descriptions are preserved in official language, often in detached bureaucratic tone.

The ethical challenge is significant:

How does one present documented brutality without reproducing its violence theatrically?

Historians who work with traumatic archives often confront this dilemma. Full sensory description may risk turning suffering into spectacle. Excessive omission risks minimizing what occurred.

This volume adopts a principled balance:

It names categories of documented abuse.

It identifies where the documentation exists.

It analyzes institutional structures.

It refrains from graphic reconstruction.

The goal is comprehension, not provocation.

The violence of the transatlantic system and its successor legal and economic frameworks is not diminished by avoiding gratuitous imagery. The evidence of its severity lies in the institutional permanence of the records themselves.

The paper trail confirms the reality.

DEFINITIONS & HISTORICAL TERMINOLOGY CLARIFICATION

The following terms appear in historical documents and academic analysis. They are included here in neutral explanatory form.

Forced Reproduction ("Breeding" in archival terminology):

A documented practice in which enslaved women were compelled to bear children for the purpose of increasing labor supply. Evidence appears in plantation correspondence, property inventories, and legal disputes concerning inheritance and valuation.

Sexual Coercion & Assault:

Documented instances in court cases, plantation records, and testimony collections indicating the use of power to compel sexual activity without consent.

Lynching:

Extrajudicial killing, often public, documented in coroner reports, newspaper accounts, and federal investigations.

Trafficking:

The forced transport and sale of individuals through maritime or domestic trade systems, evidenced in shipping manifests, bills of sale, and insurance claims.

Buck Breaking (historical terminology):

A term appearing in some historical discussions to describe coercive acts intended to psychologically dominate individuals through public humiliation. Scholars debate the documentation and prevalence of this term; references appear in both oral histories and some interpretive analyses.

Medical Exploitation:

Documented use of marginalized populations in medical experimentation or research without informed consent. Evidence exists in medical journals, hospital archives, and congressional investigations.

These terms are not presented to sensationalize history. They are presented because they appear in the documentary record.

Understanding their meaning is necessary for interpreting the archival evidence responsibly.

CLOSING NOTE ON SCOPE AND FUTURE CONTINUATION

This edition is intentionally restrained.

The archival record contains details that are more explicit, more personal, and more devastating than what is presented here. Scholars who access the primary materials will encounter language that is direct, unfiltered, and, at times, overwhelming.

There is an argument to be made one that future volumes may explore, that a full accounting of this past requires confronting the raw detail preserved in those files. Not to sensationalize, but to ensure that minimization never replaces truth.

This book lays the structural foundation.

A more detailed continuation may be necessary for those prepared to examine the unedited archive in full depth.

History, when fully revealed, demands both courage and discipline.

This volume provides the discipline.

The courage may be required next.

Introduction

History did not forget.

It was written.

Not whispered.

Not imagined.

Not guessed.

Recorded.

In ink that dried centuries ago.

In ledgers bound with twine.

In courtrooms where verdicts echoed like iron doors closing.

In manifests signed by men who never saw themselves as villains.

Some truths survive not because they were protected,

but because they were documented.

This book is not built on rumor.

It is built on paper.

Paper that lists names beside prices.

Paper that cataloged bodies beside cargo.

Paper that counted human beings the way merchants counted barrels, livestock, or coin.

There exist records that show exactly how systems of domination functioned, how they were legalized, how they were normalized, and how they were enforced. They were not hidden. They were filed. Preserved. Indexed.

And that is what makes them powerful.

Because when a crime is written down by the very people committing it, denial becomes impossible.

For generations, many believed the worst atrocities of history must have been exaggerated. Surely, they said, the stories were dramatized. Surely, memory made things harsher than they truly were.

But archives do not exaggerate.

They catalog.

Ledgers do not speculate.

They itemize.

Court records do not imagine.

They testify.

Inside those records lies a reality more chilling than legend: systems so structured, so organized, and so legally reinforced that exploitation became procedure, cruelty became policy, and human suffering became administration.

This book does not aim to shock.

It aims to reveal.

Not through accusation.

Through evidence.

Not through outrage.

Through documentation.

What you will encounter in these pages are not tales passed down through rumor or folklore. They are drawn from preserved testimony, official filings, shipping logs, legal transcripts, sworn statements, and government records, documents created in real time by the very institutions that operated these systems.

They did not think anyone centuries later would read them with moral clarity.

They assumed the world would forget.

But paper does not forget.

Ink does not forget.

Records do not forget.

And once seen, they cannot be unseen.

You are about to read what history wrote when it thought no one was looking.

Chapter One

Chapter 1 When Human Worth Was Written in Currency

THE PRICE OF A BODY

The room was quiet.

Not the quiet of peace,

the quiet of transaction.

A wooden table stood at the center, its surface worn smooth by decades of use. Papers lay stacked in careful order. Ink bottles. Ledgers. A scale for weighing coins. A clerk seated with a quill poised above parchment.

No chains clattered.

No voices cried out.

No violence was visible.

Yet what happened in rooms like this reshaped continents.

Because this was where a human life was given a price.

THE DOCUMENT THAT REDUCED A PERSON TO NUMBERS

In archives across the United States and Europe survive thousands of preserved auction sheets, probate inventories, and estate settlements from the eighteenth and nineteenth centuries. These were not secret documents. They were legal instruments required for commerce.

They look mundane.

Each line contains, name (sometimes), age, sex, occupation or skill. condition, and value.

One surviving probate inventory from Georgia, dated 1828, lists human beings alongside farm tools and livestock. The format does not distinguish between them. A plow is listed. A horse is listed. A man is listed. Each followed by a monetary value.

No commentary appears in the record.

No justification.

No apology.

Only numbers.

Historians examining such inventories, preserved today in state archives and university collections, note that these documents were created not for cruelty but for accounting. Estates had to be valued for inheritance and taxation. The law required precision.

So clerks measured human lives the way merchants measured property.

WHEN LAW DEFINED VALUE

The legal framework that allowed these documents to exist was not accidental. Colonial and early American statutes explicitly codified enslaved persons as property.

The Virginia statute of 1705, preserved in legislative records, declared enslaved individuals to be classified legally as "real estate." This meant they could be:

inherited

seized for debt

mortgaged

transferred....

In practical terms, a person could be used as collateral.

Banks recorded such transactions. Loan agreements survive showing individuals pledged as security for repayment. These contracts are held today in historical manuscript collections, some written in elegant cursive script on thick rag paper.

They read like any financial agreement.

Except for the line describing what would be forfeited if payment failed.

THE AUCTION BLOCK AS MARKETPLACE

Newspaper advertisements from the eighteenth and nineteenth centuries, many digitized in the Library of Congress's Chronicling America database, contain notices placed by sellers.

The language is striking not for its brutality, but for its calm.

One advertisement from 1769 announces:

"To be sold: a healthy Negro boy, about fourteen years of age..."

Another lists:

"A woman, strong and accustomed to field work..."

The tone resembles classified ads for livestock or equipment. The phrasing is polite, concise, businesslike.

Because in the legal system that produced them, these notices were ordinary commerce.

THE INSURANCE OF HUMAN CARGO

Perhaps no surviving document reveals the logic of commodification more starkly than maritime insurance records.

Merchants routinely insured enslaved Africans during transatlantic voyages, just as they insured ships or goods. Insurance contracts, preserved in British archival collections, assigned monetary value to each person aboard.

This practice became infamous in a case historians still study:

Gregson v. Gilbert (1783)

After more than one hundred enslaved Africans died aboard the ship Zong, the owners filed an insurance claim seeking compensation for lost cargo. Court transcripts show the legal debate focused on whether the deaths qualified as a reimbursable loss.

The central legal question was not:

Were lives unjustly taken?

It was:

Was the property loss covered?

The distinction is chilling not because it was hidden, but because it was written plainly.

THE SILENT LANGUAGE OF RECORDS

Documents do not shout.

They do not accuse.

They do something far more powerful,

They remain.

Each surviving ledger, advertisement, and contract is a fragment of a larger system, a system that functioned not through chaos but through organization. The machinery of exploitation did not operate in darkness. It operated in offices, courts, ports, banks, and counting rooms.

It had procedures.

It had rules.

It had paperwork.

And paperwork leaves evidence.

WHAT SHOCKS HISTORIANS MOST

Modern readers often expect historical atrocities to be recorded with outrage. Instead, historians consistently observe the opposite.

The more normalized a practice was in its own time, the more routine its documentation appears.

Clerks who recorded prices did not describe suffering.

Insurance agents did not describe fear.

Auctioneers did not describe grief.

They described value.

Because value was what the system required them to see.

THE LASTING POWER OF WRITTEN PROOF

Stories can be doubted.

Memories can be disputed.

But records, especially those created by the system itself, carry a different authority.

They testify against their own authors.

Not intentionally. Inevitably.

Every preserved document is a witness that never forgets what it saw.

END OF CHAPTER LINE

A chain can be broken.

A law can be repealed.

A system can collapse.

But once a price is written beside a human name, history remembers that it happened.

END OF CHAPTER ANALYSIS

Law, Classification, and the Meaning of the Record

The preceding account is not presented only as narrative history. It is presented as documentary history, history preserved through records created by the very institutions that governed the events described.

At first glance, the incident may appear to be an isolated historical episode. But when examined through a legal lens, it becomes something else entirely: a case study in how systems of authority classify human life.

Because in law, classification determines consequence.

A court does not simply ask what happened.

It asks what category the event belongs to.

That distinction changes everything.

I. LEGAL CLASSIFICATION AND OUTCOME

Legal systems function through categories. Whether an event is defined as:

crime

accident

loss

contract dispute

Or civil claim

determines which court hears it, which rules apply, and what remedies exist.

When human beings are classified within property law rather than personhood law, the legal consequences shift dramatically. Criminal liability may vanish. Civil liability may replace it. Moral judgment becomes legally irrelevant.

This is not theoretical. It is procedural.

Law follows classification.

II. WHAT MODERN LEGAL STANDARDS RECOGNIZE

Under contemporary legal doctrine, systems that treat human beings as commercial property would violate fundamental principles now recognized across constitutional, statutory, and international law, including:

equal protection of the law

due process rights

prohibitions against involuntary servitude

protections against cruel or degrading treatment

basic human rights doctrines

Modern law distinguishes sharply between property and personhood. That distinction is foundational.

The historical systems examined in this chapter existed before many of those principles were codified or enforced. Their documentation therefore reveals not only past conditions, but the legal evolution required to change them.

III. SYSTEMS, NOT INCIDENTS

The significance of the records described in this chapter is not limited to what occurred. Their deeper importance lies in what they show about institutional structure.

Individual wrongdoing is one category of historical event.

Institutional authorization is another.

When documentation shows that procedures were followed, filings made, claims submitted, and decisions issued through official channels, the historical focus shifts from individual actors to systemic operation.

That shift is essential for accurate analysis.

IV. CONTINUITY AND CHANGE

Historical comparison requires precision. It is neither accurate nor responsible to claim that past conditions are identical to the present. Laws change. Institutions reform. Legal protections expand.

However, historians and legal scholars often analyze continuity at the level of structure rather than surface conditions.

They ask:

Do administrative mechanisms persist?

Do discretionary powers remain?

Do classification systems still shape outcomes?

Ask these questions honestly to yourself...........

Structural continuity does not mean identical conditions. It means certain institutional mechanisms may endure even as laws evolve.

Recognizing that distinction prevents oversimplification while preserving analytical clarity.

V. WHY THE ARCHIVE MATTERS

Archival records are uniquely powerful historical sources because they were not created to persuade future readers. They were created to conduct official business at the time.

They therefore reveal how systems actually operated, not how later generations imagined they operated.

This is why courts, legislatures, commissions, and scholars repeatedly return to primary documentation when evaluating historical questions.

Records are evidence.

Evidence allows analysis.

Analysis allows understanding.

LEGAL REFLECTION (to author's personal understanding and extent, without degrees or said paperwork)

What is documented cannot be dismissed as rumor.

What is recorded cannot be reduced to legend.

The file does not argue.

The ledger does not exaggerate.

The record does not speculate.

It states.

And when institutions themselves create the record, that record becomes one of the most powerful forms of historical proof available.

FINAL CHAPTER TRANSITION

The events described in this chapter are preserved not because they were remembered, but because they were written.

Clerks entered them.

Courts filed them.

Institutions stored them.

And once recorded, they became part of the permanent archive.

What follows are the primary documentary sources through which readers may examine the surviving record for themselves.

PRIMARY SOURCE REFERENCES FOR THIS CHAPTER

(Readers can verify independently)

Virginia Slave Code (1705) — Colonial legislative archives

Probate inventories (18th–19th c.) — State archive collections

Chronicling America newspaper database — Library of Congress

British National Archives maritime insurance records

Gregson v. Gilbert (1783) court records

Chapter Two

Chapter 2 THE SHIPS THAT WROTE THEIR OWN EVIDENCE

Ledgers from the Ocean Floor of History

Before they reached shore, they were counted. Not welcomed. Not greeted, Counted.

Long before any auction block, courtroom, or plantation record, there existed another archive, one that traveled across oceans, written in ink that smelled faintly of salt and iron.

The ships wrote first.

THE FLOATING FILE CABINETS

Inside maritime archives in London, Lisbon, Seville, Amsterdam, and Boston are preserved thousands of shipping logs from transatlantic voyages. At first glance they resemble ordinary merchant records. They contain the same columns as any trading vessel ledger:

departure port, cargo type, quantity, loss, And arrival date.

But in certain logs, one category appears that alters everything:

"Negroes embarked."

This phrase appears repeatedly in preserved documents from the Trans-Atlantic Slave Trade Database, a modern research project compiled from over 35,000 documented voyages using original ship records, customs logs, and port registries.

Each entry is not a story. It is a statistic.

And statistics do something narrative cannot, They reveal scale.

THE LANGUAGE OF NUMBERS AT SEA

A typical eighteenth-century ship log might list:

312 embarked

276 arrived

No explanation follows.

No narrative describes what happened between those numbers. The ledger assumes no explanation is necessary. It records only the figures because figures are what merchants required.

Historians who study these documents often note a chilling feature, the entries are written in steady handwriting, without interruption, as though the writer were recording grain shipments or barrels of rum.

Which, in legal terms, is precisely what they were doing.

The law defined human cargo as goods. The logbook obeyed the law.

A SHIP'S JOURNAL AS COURT TESTIMONY

Unlike rumor or oral tradition, shipping records were legal instruments. Captains were required to keep them. Ports demanded them. Investors relied on them. Courts accepted them as evidence.

This requirement unintentionally produced one of the most detailed documentary trails in human history.

Because every voyage had to account for its cargo.

The result:

Ships became witnesses.

They recorded:

how many boarded

how many survived

how many were lost

Not emotionally.

Administratively.

THE MORTALITY COLUMN

Among the most studied entries in slave ship logs is a single column labeled:

Loss, Sometimes the number is small.

Sometimes it is not.

Modern historians analyzing British Admiralty and Royal African Company records have confirmed that mortality rates varied widely but were consistently tracked with precision. Investors wanted accurate accounting. Death represented financial loss.

And so death was recorded.

Not mourned.

Recorded.

THE CASE THAT SHOCKED HISTORIANS

One of the most cited maritime cases in archival research is preserved in British legal history:

The Ship Zong

— 1781

The surviving documentation of this voyage includes court transcripts, insurance filings, and merchant correspondence.

These records confirm that when the ship reached Jamaica, its owners filed an insurance claim for lost cargo. The dispute became the case Gregson v. Gilbert (1783).

The legal arguments preserved in court archives focus almost entirely on contractual liability and insurance coverage.

The central legal question:

Was the loss financially compensable?

The court debated shipping law, maritime precedent, and contractual obligation. The surviving transcript shows almost no discussion of the moral dimension.

Not because no one cared.

Because the legal system had already categorized the matter as commercial.

THE MAP THAT NO ONE EXPECTED

Today, researchers can visualize transatlantic voyages using digitized archival shipping data. When plotted geographically, these routes form dense lines stretching from African ports to the Americas.

Seen together, they resemble something unexpected:

A network.

Not random journeys.

Not isolated incidents.

A system.

Historians analyzing these maps emphasize that the trade was not chaotic piracy. It was structured commerce supported by governments, banks, insurers, and shipping companies.

Ships were not rogue actors.

They were participants in a regulated economy.

WHAT THE OCEAN DID NOT ERASE

Water erases footprints.

It dissolves ink.

It swallows wreckage.

But it cannot erase documents stored on land.

Even when ships vanished, records often remained in port registries, insurance ledgers, customs offices, and merchant account books. This is why historians can reconstruct voyages centuries later with remarkable precision.

The ocean buried the vessels.

The archives preserved the evidence.

WHY THESE RECORDS MATTER

When people speak about history, they often argue about interpretation. Perspectives differ. Narratives clash.

But shipping logs are not interpretations.

They are measurements.

They do not tell us what someone felt.

They tell us what someone counted.

And counting is difficult to dispute.

THE SILENT TESTIMONY OF INK

The clerks who wrote these entries did not think they were documenting history. They believed they were performing routine duties. Recording numbers. Completing forms. Filing reports.

Yet those ordinary actions created an extraordinary archive.

Because bureaucracy remembers what individuals forget.

The ships are gone.

The captains are gone.

The merchants are gone.

But the ink remains.

Storms may sink vessels.

Time may erase voices.

But once a voyage is written down, it never stops arriving.

END OF CHAPTER ANALYSIS

Commerce, Documentation, and the Legal Language of Ships

The ships described in this chapter did more than cross oceans. They generated records.

Every voyage produced paperwork. Every transaction created entries. Every decision left traces in ink. Long after wood decayed and sails vanished, the documentation remained.

This is what distinguishes maritime systems of the era from later myths about them:

They were not undocumented operations.

They were administrative enterprises.

I. THE SHIP AS A LEGAL ENTITY

Under maritime law, a ship was not merely a vehicle. It functioned as a recognized legal unit capable of:

carrying contracts

holding insurance value

being registered property

appearing in court proceedings

Because ships were regulated commercial instruments, their voyages required detailed recording. That requirement generated extensive documentation, including:

manifests

insurance filings

ownership registries

crew logs

cargo inventories

These records were created not for historians, but for enforcement, accounting, and litigation.

II. WHEN COMMERCE CREATES EVIDENCE

Commercial systems demand documentation. Without records, claims cannot be settled, losses cannot be calculated, and ownership cannot be proven.

For that reason, maritime commerce produced one of the most detailed paper trails in early modern history.

Insurance companies required written proof.

Courts required written filings.

Ports required written declarations.

As a result, ships effectively documented themselves.

Their logs became testimony.

Their manifests became ledgers.

Their registries became archives.

III. LEGAL LANGUAGE VS. HUMAN REALITY

One of the most striking features of maritime documentation is the language used in official records. Legal and commercial terminology often reduced complex human realities into administrative categories.

This transformation was not accidental. It was procedural.

Administrative systems rely on standardized terminology because standardized terminology allows processing. Once events are translated into bureaucratic language, they can be filed, assessed, and adjudicated.

The law does not operate through emotion. It operates through classification....... When the law operates lawfully.....

IV. WHY THESE RECORDS MATTER TODAY

Maritime archives remain among the most detailed historical sources available to researchers. They are relied upon by:

courts evaluating historical claims

scholars reconstructing economic systems

genealogists tracing lineage

policymakers examining institutional development

Because these records were created contemporaneously with the voyages themselves, they are considered primary evidence. Their value lies not only in what they describe, but in the fact that they were written at the moment events occurred.

In historical research, proximity to the event strengthens evidentiary weight.

V. SYSTEMS LEAVE PAPER TRAILS

A system that operates informally leaves rumors.

A system that operates formally leaves files.

The maritime world described in this chapter belonged to the second category. It functioned through registration, certification, notarization, and verification. Those processes generated documentation that survives centuries later.

The existence of that documentation demonstrates that these voyages were not peripheral activities. They were integrated into commercial and legal frameworks recognized by states and institutions.

LEGAL REFLECTION

Ships do not testify.

Records do.

Wood rots. Iron corrodes. Sailcloth disappears.

But ink endures.

And when a system writes its own records, it preserves the evidence of how it operated, whether or not it intended that evidence to be read generations later.

FINAL CHAPTER TRANSITION

The vessels are gone.

The oceans are silent.

The routes are empty.

Yet the record remains.

What survives is not the ship, but the documentation the ship was required to produce.

Those documents still exist, stored in archives, registries, and repositories across the world.

Institutions and the Appearance of Procedure

One of the most revealing patterns in historical records is the presence of procedure. Formal steps create the appearance of order, and order creates the appearance of legitimacy. When actions are processed through official channels, they can appear lawful even when their effects raise profound questions.

Procedure is powerful because it does not rely on force. It relies on form. A stamped document, a signed form, or a filed report can carry authority precisely because it looks routine.

Routine, however, can normalize extraordinary outcomes.

The seal made it official.

The signature made it binding.

The file made it permanent.

Procedure can transform action into policy.

The paperwork generated by these procedures still exists, preserved in boxes, folders, and record groups across archival institutions. Each document is a fragment of a larger administrative structure.Those fragments remain accessible.

The act passed.

The record stayed.

The following section presents the primary sources through which readers may examine that surviving record directly.

PRIMARY SOURCE DOSSIER — VERIFIED ARCHIVES

Readers can independently consult:

Trans-Atlantic Slave Trade Database (Emory University) — compiled from original ship logs and port records

British National Archives — Admiralty and maritime insurance records

Gregson v. Gilbert (1783) — British court case transcript

Royal African Company shipping logs — manuscript collections

Customs port registries (17th–19th c.) — European and American archives

Chapter Three

Chapter 3 The Systems That Replaced Them

When the chains were removed, the paperwork increased.

That is the first detail historians notice when they study the decades after emancipation. Contrary to popular imagination, the end of slavery did not produce a disappearance of control systems. It produced a transformation of them, one that left a paper trail thicker than before.

Because once slavery became illegal, domination required something new:

Justification.

And justification always generates documents.

THE FIRST FILES OF FREEDOM

In 1865, the United States government established the Freedmen's Bureau, formally known as the Bureau of Refugees, Freedmen, and

Abandoned Lands. Today, its records are preserved in the U.S. National Archives.

Inside these files are:

labor contracts

assault reports

kidnapping complaints

wage disputes

court petitions

These were not rumors. They were sworn filings.

Many describe newly freed individuals attempting to claim wages that had been promised but never paid. Others report violence used to force labor after emancipation. Some detail attempts to illegally re-enslave freed people through coercion or fabricated charges.

Historians examining these documents often remark on a striking pattern:

Freedom had been declared.

Control had not ended.

THE LAW AS A REPLACEMENT CHAIN

After the Civil War, Southern legislatures enacted a set of statutes commonly called Black Codes. These laws survive today in state legislative archives and legal collections.

Their provisions varied by state but often included penalties for:

vagrancy

loitering

unemployment

breach of labor contract

On paper, these laws were neutral.

In practice, arrest records preserved in county courthouses show they were overwhelmingly applied to newly freed Black citizens.

Once arrested, individuals could be fined.

If they could not pay the fine, court records show they could be:

leased to private employers until the debt was "worked off."

This system became known as convict leasing.

THE CONTRACTS THAT SOLD LABOR AGAIN

Convict leasing agreements, many preserved in state archives such as Alabama, Mississippi, and Georgia, show state governments leasing prisoners to private companies for labor.

These contracts list:

number of prisoners supplied

duration of lease

price per person

Some surviving documents specify penalties companies would pay if a leased prisoner escaped or died.

The language resembles shipping insurance contracts from centuries earlier.

Not because history repeated itself.

Because administrative logic tends to resemble itself across time.

THE INVESTIGATION THAT EXPOSED IT

One of the most important federal documents of the late nineteenth century is the Report of the U.S. Department of Justice Peonage Investigations (1901–1908).

These files, preserved in National Archives Record Group 60, contain sworn testimony from individuals forced into labor through threats, violence, or fabricated debts.

Investigators documented cases in which employers:

falsified charges

manipulated local courts

imposed impossible debts

prevented workers from leaving

These were not isolated accusations.

They were federal cases.

THE PATTERN HISTORIANS IDENTIFY

Modern scholars studying post-Civil War records consistently identify a structural pattern:

When one system of control became illegal, another system appeared that functioned differently in law but similarly in effect.

Not identical.

But comparable in outcome.

This observation does not come from speculation.

It comes from documents.

WHY THESE RECORDS ARE LESS KNOWN

The records exist.

They are preserved.

They are accessible.

Yet many remain unfamiliar to the public.

Not because they were hidden, but because they are scattered across:

county courthouses

state archives

legal record groups

microfilm collections

And academic repositories

Unlike famous historical documents displayed in museums, these papers were administrative. Routine. Technical. Filed away after use.

They were never meant to be dramatic.

Which is precisely why they are so revealing.

THE ARCHIVE'S QUIET CONFESSION

Oppressive systems rarely describe themselves as oppressive. Instead, they describe themselves as lawful.

And lawful systems generate documentation.

Every arrest creates a record.

Every contract creates a file.

Every prosecution creates a transcript.

Over time, these papers accumulate.

Eventually, they form a record too large to ignore.

Freedom changed the law.

But the archives show it did not immediately change power.

END OF CHAPTER ANALYSIS

Institutional Continuity and Legal Transformation

The evidence examined in this chapter demonstrates that institutional systems do not simply disappear when laws change. Instead, they are often restructured through new statutes, administrative procedures, and regulatory frameworks. The legal record shows that transitions are typically managed through formal mechanisms rather than abrupt endings.

Modern legal analysis recognizes this phenomenon as structural continuity, the persistence of administrative logic even when legal language evolves. Studying such continuity does not assume equivalence between past and present. It examines how institutions adapt over time and how authority reorganizes itself within changing legal environments.

The documents preserved in archives provide direct evidence of these transitions. They reveal not only what systems existed, but how they were redesigned.

LEGAL REFLECTION

Systems rarely vanish.

They are revised.

They are renamed.

And the archive remembers every version.

FINAL TRANSITION

The transformation described in this chapter is preserved not in memory but in documentation. Legislative volumes, administrative files, and procedural manuals still exist, cataloged and accessible to researchers.

They can be examined.

The system changed its form.

The record kept its shape.

VERIFIED ARCHIVAL SOURCES FOR THIS CHAPTER

Readers can independently research:

Freedmen's Bureau Records — U.S. National Archives (Record Group 105)

Black Codes — state legislative archives (1865–1867)

Convict Leasing Contracts — Alabama State Archives & similar collections

DOJ Peonage Case Files — National Archives RG 60

Congressional Reports on Peonage (early 1900s)

STRATEGIC NOTE (Author Level Insight)

Shifting your book toward post-slavery documentation is extremely powerful because:

it is less commonly covered

it relies heavily on primary sources

it challenges simplified historical timelines

it keeps readers intellectually engaged

This is exactly the approach used by bestselling investigative history writers.

Chapter Four

Chapter 4 THE COURTROOM WITHOUT A JURY

When Justice Was Written but Not Delivered

The room looked official.

That is what witnesses remembered.

Wooden benches.

A raised bench for the judge.

A clerk with a ledger.

A flag.

A seal.

Everything about it resembled justice.

That was the design......

Because systems of power rarely present themselves as unjust. They present themselves as procedure.

And procedure has a script.

THE PROMISE OF EQUALITY IN INK

In 1868, the Fourteenth Amendment to the United States Constitution was ratified. Its language, preserved in the National Archives, declared that no state could deny any person:

"the equal protection of the laws."

On paper, this sentence changed everything.

In practice, court records show that its enforcement depended entirely on who controlled the courtroom.

WHEN LAW EXISTS BUT PROTECTION DOES NOT

Across southern county courthouses in the late nineteenth century, surviving case dockets reveal a pattern historians have studied for decades: criminal cases involving violence against Black citizens often stalled, disappeared, or ended without prosecution.

Not secretly.

Documented.

Scholars analyzing state court archives in Mississippi, Georgia, and Louisiana have found entries listing charges filed, followed by notations such as:

dismissed

insufficient evidence

no bill returned

Many of these entries appear without explanation.

The clerk wrote the result.

The system moved on.

THE CASE FILES THAT SURVIVED

One of the most studied federal investigations into post-Civil War violence appears in the records of the U.S. Department of Justice

Civil Rights Prosecutions (1870s), preserved today in the National Archives.

These files contain sworn testimony describing intimidation, assaults, and killings reported by newly freed citizens.

They also contain something else:

Evidence of failed prosecutions.

In numerous cases, federal prosecutors documented that local juries refused to convict defendants even when testimony was presented.

The transcripts remain.

They do not speculate.

They record.

JURIES THAT NEVER CONVENED

The absence of a jury can be as revealing as its verdict.

Historians studying court ledgers from Reconstruction-era counties have identified multiple entries where indictments were filed but no trial followed. Some records note:

"No jury assembled."

Others list:

"Witnesses unavailable."

These brief notations, written in ordinary handwriting, mask extraordinary realities. Witnesses sometimes disappeared. In other cases, individuals declined to testify out of fear.

The record rarely explains why.

It simply notes that proceedings ended.

THE SLAUGHTERHOUSE DECISION

One of the most consequential Supreme Court rulings affecting post-slavery justice is preserved in the official United States Reports:

The Slaughterhouse Cases (1873)

This decision narrowed the scope of federal protections under the Fourteenth Amendment. Legal historians widely agree that the ruling limited the federal government's ability to intervene when states failed to protect citizens' rights.

The opinion itself is not hidden. It is published, indexed, and studied in law schools.

Its consequences appear not in theory, but in subsequent case records showing reduced federal prosecution of civil rights violations.

The ruling did not remove rights from paper.

It weakened their enforcement in practice.

WHAT COURT DOCUMENTS REVEAL ABOUT POWER

Modern readers often assume injustice is obvious. But archival court records show something subtler: injustice frequently operates through absence rather than action.

Cases not filed.

Charges not pursued.

Witnesses not called.

Juries not seated.

Each absence leaves a mark.

Because absence, when recorded, becomes evidence.

THE FEDERAL INVESTIGATORS WHO WROTE IT DOWN

In the early twentieth century, federal investigators documented forced labor and coercion cases in what are now known as the Peonage Files (National Archives Record Group 60).

These files include sworn statements describing situations in which individuals were prevented from leaving employment through threats or fabricated debts.

Some cases resulted in prosecutions.

Many did not.

But whether or not convictions occurred, the reports remain.

Typed. Filed. Preserved.

THE QUIET POWER OF CLERKS

Historians often note an overlooked figure in historical documentation: the clerk.

Not the judge.

Not the lawyer.

Not the politician.

The clerk.

Clerks recorded outcomes without commentary. They did not argue cases or interpret laws. They wrote what happened.

Because they wrote it, we can read it!

And because we can read it, the system that produced those outcomes can still be studied today.

WHY THESE FILES MATTER NOW

Records from post-slavery court systems demonstrate something essential about institutional power:

A law can exist.

A right can be declared.

A protection can be promised.

But only enforcement determines whether those words live or remain ink.

The archives do not claim this.

They show it.......

A courtroom can look like justice.

But history is written by what happens after the gavel falls.

END OF CHAPTER ANALYSIS

Authority, Classification, and the Architecture of Control

The material examined in this chapter reveals that systems of authority rarely operate through force alone. Their most enduring power lies in their ability to define categories. Once a classification is created within official records, it can determine treatment, jurisdiction, access, and limitation.

Classification is not merely descriptive. It is administrative.

Legal and institutional structures rely on categories because categories allow decisions to be standardized. Standardization, in turn, allows authority to operate efficiently across large populations. A label entered into a ledger or registry does not simply describe an individual; it can determine how the system interacts with that individual.

This is why classification systems appear repeatedly in archival records. They were necessary tools for governance, and because they were necessary, they were documented. The surviving files demonstrate that these categories were not incidental. They were deliberate components of administrative design.

LEGAL REFLECTION

To define is to direct.

To record is to enforce.

A category written once can outlast the moment that created it.

FINAL TRANSITION

The classifications described in this chapter did not vanish when the moment passed. They were entered into registries, copied into reports, and preserved in institutional archives. What remains today is not rumor, but record, documentation that allows later generations to study how systems organized authority through language.

Those records still exist!!!

The label was assigned.

History carried it forward.

PRIMARY SOURCE DOSSIER — VERIFIED RECORDS

Readers may consult:

Reconstruction-era federal prosecution records — U.S. National Archives

Department of Justice Peonage Files — RG 60

County court dockets (1870–1900) — state archives

The Slaughterhouse Cases (1873) — U.S. Supreme Court Reports

Congressional Reconstruction reports — Library of Congress

Chapter Five

Chapter 5 THE CONTRACTS OF CONTROL

When Freedom Was Signed Away in Ink

Freedom did not arrive alone.

It arrived carrying paper.

Not chains.

Not shackles.

Contracts.

Because when ownership of bodies became illegal, ownership of labor became the next battleground, and labor, unlike chains, could be bound with signatures.

THE FIRST SIGNATURES OF "FREE" LABOR

After the Civil War, thousands of formerly enslaved men and women entered into written labor agreements. These documents still exist today in the preserved records of the Freedmen's Bureau (National Archives Record Group 105).

They are orderly forms, often handwritten, sometimes printed with blank spaces filled in by ink. They typically list:

employer name

worker name

duration of service

wages promised

penalties for violation

On the surface, they appear to represent progress: a contractual agreement between employer and employee.

But historians who analyze these contracts note something unusual.

The obligations were not equal.

Many contracts required workers to:

remain on a plantation for a full year

obey employer orders

request permission to leave property

forfeit wages for rule violations

In contrast, penalties for employers were often absent.

The contract did not need chains.

The contract was the restraint.

THE FINE PRINT THAT DEFINED POWER

One preserved Mississippi contract dated 1866 includes a clause stating that workers who left before the end of the term would:

"forfeit all wages due."

Another requires laborers to supply their own food and clothing despite earning wages too small to reasonably do so.

Historians studying these agreements emphasize that they were technically legal documents. They were filed, witnessed, and sometimes notarized.

The system did not operate outside the law.

It operated through it.

THE DEBT THAT COULD NOT BE PAID

Many post-emancipation labor systems relied on debt accounting, and surviving plantation ledgers demonstrate how it worked.

Workers were advanced supplies, tools, food, clothing, housing costs, recorded as charges against future wages. Account books preserved in university manuscript collections show itemized deductions such as:

seed

meal

cloth

doctor's visit

mule rental

At the end of a season, totals were calculated.

In numerous surviving ledgers, the result is the same:

Balance owed.... (Reminiscent of TODAY!)

The worker did not receive payment.

Instead, the worker owed money.

Debt became a tether.

THE LEGALITY OF DEPENDENCE

This system, often called sharecropping, is widely documented in agricultural account books, county registries, and private estate records from the late nineteenth century.

It was not secret.

It was standard.

Farmers who entered such agreements frequently had no access to independent markets, credit institutions, or land ownership. Surviving economic reports from the U.S. Department of Agriculture in the late 1800s show how widespread this arrangement became across the South.

Historians analyzing these reports describe a cycle:

contract → debt → renewed contract

Each year the ledger closed.

Each year the ledger reopened.

THE COURT RECORDS OF DISPUTE

Freedmen's Bureau court files include disputes filed by workers claiming unpaid wages or unfair treatment. These petitions survive in thousands of pages of testimony.

Many follow a similar pattern:

A worker states wages were promised.

The employer disputes the amount.

The clerk records both statements.

Sometimes a judgment appears in the margin.

Sometimes there is only silence.

Because not every case reached resolution.

But every case was documented.

WHEN AGREEMENT BECOMES OBLIGATION

Modern readers often assume contracts imply fairness. Yet legal historians emphasize that a contract reflects power relationships at the moment it is signed.

When one party controls land, food, tools, and law enforcement, and the other controls only their labor, the contract does not represent equal negotiation.

It represents available options.

And sometimes, available options are few.

THE PAPER TRAIL THAT SURVIVED

What makes these systems historically undeniable is not oral tradition or later interpretation. It is the surviving paper trail.

Contracts preserved.

Ledgers archived.

Petitions filed.

Accounts totaled.

The individuals who created these documents did not intend them to become historical evidence. They were conducting routine business.

But routine paperwork accumulates.

And accumulation creates record.

WHAT HISTORIANS SEE IN THE PATTERN

When scholars compare labor contracts from the 1860s to plantation inventories from the 1850s, they often observe a structural shift rather than a total break.

The terminology changed.

The legal framework changed.

But the dependence often remained.

This conclusion is not drawn from ideology.

It is drawn from documents.

Chains bind the body.

Contracts bind the future.

And the archives remember both.

END OF CHAPTER ANALYSIS

Procedure, Legitimacy, and the Power of Form

The records examined in this chapter demonstrate a central principle of institutional history: authority often operates most effectively when it appears routine. Systems that rely on procedure rather than spectacle rarely draw immediate attention, yet they can exert profound influence over outcomes.

Procedure gives action structure. Structure gives action legitimacy. And legitimacy, once documented, can transform decisions into accepted policy. This is why official processes, forms, signatures, seals, filings, approvals, appear so frequently in archival material. They were not decorative elements. They were mechanisms.

When an action passes through recognized channels, it acquires institutional force. The presence of documentation signals that a decision was not accidental but processed. That distinction is critical for legal interpretation, because systems of law often evaluate conduct not only by what occurred, but by whether it occurred within authorized procedure.

In this way, form can shape reality. A stamped document may carry more authority than a spoken statement. A filed report may outweigh testimony. A completed form may determine jurisdiction. The archive reveals that procedural systems do not merely record decisions, they enable them.

LEGAL REFLECTION

Procedure rarely raises its voice.

It signs.

It stamps.

It files.

And once filed, it governs.

FINAL TRANSITION

The documents discussed in this chapter remain preserved in repositories, record groups, and institutional collections. Their language is administrative, their tone routine, yet their implications are lasting. They show how systems functioned not through dramatic moments, but through repeated acts of documentation.

Those records can still be read.

The process looked ordinary.

The consequences were not.

PRIMARY SOURCE DOSSIER — VERIFIED ARCHIVAL RECORDS

Readers can independently research:

Freedmen's Bureau Labor Contracts — National Archives RG 105

Sharecropping account ledgers — Southern Historical Collection (UNC), Duke Archives, LSU Special Collections

Post-Civil War agricultural reports — U.S. Department of Agriculture historical bulletins

Freedmen's Bureau Court Records — digital collections (FamilySearch / National Archives)

Reconstruction labor dispute files — Library of Congress manuscript collections

Chapter Six

Chapter 6
THE CHARGES THAT CREATED PRISONERS

When Arrest Became a Labor Supply

The chain did not disappear.

It changed hands.

Where it had once been fastened by private owners, it was now fastened by the state. Not always visibly. Not always violently. Often it was fastened by something quieter:

A charge.

Because an accusation, once written into a ledger, can restrain a person as effectively as iron.

THE NEW ARREST RECORDS

After the Civil War, county arrest logs across the American South began to fill rapidly. These logs still exist in courthouse archives, many preserved on microfilm or in state historical collections. Their pages look ordinary: columns, dates, names, charges.

But historians who study these documents have long noted a striking pattern.

The charges that appear most frequently include:

vagrancy

loitering

disorderly conduct

breach of contract

"idle behavior"

Such offenses required no victim. They required only accusation.

The wording appears neutral.

The application often was not.

THE VAGRANCY STATUTES

Among the earliest post-emancipation legal tools were vagrancy laws, enacted in several states beginning in 1865. These statutes, preserved in legislative archives, defined criminal behavior in unusually broad terms.

In some jurisdictions, a person could be arrested if they could not demonstrate proof of employment or residence.

Court records show how these laws operated in practice. Arrest dockets from Reconstruction-era counties list individuals charged with vagrancy and fined amounts they could not pay.

And fines created a new mechanism of control.

Because unpaid fines had consequences.

THE FINE THAT BECAME A SENTENCE

If a defendant could not pay a fine, local courts often converted that fine into labor. This process is documented in county sentencing records and state penitentiary registers preserved today in archival collections.

The notation appears frequently:

"Fine unpaid, committed."

Once committed, the individual could be transferred into custody systems that allowed local governments to lease prisoners to private employers.

This system became known as convict leasing.

THE CONTRACTS FOR PRISON LABOR

Convict leasing agreements survive in state archives such as those of Alabama, Georgia, and Tennessee. These contracts detail arrangements between state authorities and private companies.

They list:

number of prisoners leased

duration of labor

payment to the state

responsibilities of the employer

Some even specify replacement clauses if a prisoner became unable to work.

Historians who examine these documents often remark on their tone: administrative, precise, unemotional.

They read like equipment rental agreements.

Except the inventory listed is human.

THE INVESTIGATIONS THAT CONFIRMED IT

By the late nineteenth and early twentieth centuries, federal authorities began investigating forced labor practices in the South. The resulting files are preserved in the U.S. Department of Justice Peonage Case Records (National Archives Record Group 60).

These investigations include sworn testimony describing situations in which individuals were:

arrested on minor charges

fined

unable to pay

compelled to work off debt

Some cases resulted in prosecutions. Others did not. But the records remain regardless of outcome.

Typed pages.

Signed statements.

Filed evidence.

THE ECONOMICS OF ARREST

Modern historians studying prison and labor records from this era emphasize a critical observation: incarceration could generate revenue.

State financial reports from the late nineteenth century, preserved in legislative archives, show income received from leasing prisoners to private enterprises such as:

mines

lumber camps

railroads

farms

In certain years, leasing fees constituted a significant portion of state revenue.

This did not prove conspiracy.

It demonstrated incentive.

And incentives, once written into budgets, tend to shape behavior.

THE COURTROOM AS A GATEWAY

Legal scholars examining county court transcripts from the period have identified a procedural pattern:

arrest → fine → inability to pay → labor assignment

Each step is recorded separately in different documents.

Only when the records are placed side by side does the pattern become visible.

No single file reveals the system.

The archive does.

THE CLERK'S QUIET ENTRY

The clerk who recorded these cases did not announce them as historic. He wrote a name, a charge, a disposition, and moved to the next line.

But every line remained.

Today, those entries allow historians to reconstruct entire systems of labor control using nothing more than the documents produced at the time.

Because paper, unlike memory, does not forget patterns.

WHY THESE RECORDS ARE POWERFUL

When modern readers learn about systems like convict leasing, many assume they must have been hidden operations.

The archives show otherwise.

They were documented.

Contracts were filed.

Payments were logged.

Sentences were recorded.

Nothing about them was invisible.

What made them powerful was not secrecy.

It was legality.

A chain forged in iron can be broken.

A chain written into law can last far longer.

END OF CHAPTER ANALYSIS

Records, Responsibility, and Institutional Memory

The material presented in this chapter underscores a fundamental truth about documented systems:, institutions rarely forget what they record. Administrative structures are designed to preserve information because preservation enables continuity. Files allow offices to function across years, across administrations, and across personnel changes. Without records, authority would have to begin again each time leadership shifted. With records, authority continues uninterrupted.

This continuity is not incidental. It is intentional. Archival preservation is itself a form of governance, ensuring that decisions made in one moment can influence decisions made in another. The presence of documentation therefore does more than describe past events; it extends their administrative life... (read again. The tree that sheds its leaves never changes, for they are one and the same with their roots). Don't be fooled because it looks different..,,,

In legal analysis, preserved records carry particular weight because they represent contemporaneous evidence. Courts, commissions, and scholars treat such materials as especially reliable precisely because they were created at the time decisions were made. Their value lies not only in what they say, but in when they were written.

The chapter's documents demonstrate how responsibility is often traced through paper rather than memory. Signatures, dates, and entries create chains of accountability. Even when individuals change, the record can show what actions were authorized, who approved them, and under what rules they occurred. The archive, in this sense, functions as an institutional memory that outlasts any single participant.

LEGAL REFLECTION

Memory fades.

Records persist.

What a system writes, it preserves.

What it preserves, it can be judged by.

FINAL TRANSITION

The files referenced in this chapter remain housed in archival repositories, cataloged and indexed according to the administrative systems that created them. They are not reconstructions. They are originals, documents produced in real time by the institutions they describe.

They remain available for examination.

Those who made the decisions are gone.

Their paperwork is not.

PRIMARY SOURCE DOSSIER — VERIFIED RECORDS

Readers may consult:

Reconstruction arrest logs — county courthouse archives

Black Codes & vagrancy statutes — state legislative records (1865–1870)

Convict leasing contracts — Alabama State Archives, Georgia Archives, Tennessee State Library

DOJ Peonage Case Files — National Archives RG 60

State financial reports on prison leasing revenue — legislative archives

Chapter Seven

Chapter 7
THE SCHOOLS THAT RECORDED FUTURES

When Education Became the Next Battleground

The room looked harmless.

Rows of desks.

Chalkboard dust.

Sunlight through tall windows.

Nothing about it resembled a battlefield.

Yet historians studying the decades after emancipation have repeatedly identified one of the most contested arenas of power in post-slavery America:

The classroom.

Because once physical control weakened, control over knowledge became decisive.

And knowledge leaves records.

THE FIRST SCHOOLS OF FREEDOM

In the years immediately following the Civil War, thousands of newly freed men, women, and children sought something that had long been denied to them, simple literacy.

This demand is documented extensively in Freedmen's Bureau education reports preserved in the U.S. National Archives (Record Group 105). Bureau agents recorded the rapid establishment of schools across the South, noting:

enrollment numbers

teacher assignments

supply shortages

attendance rates

Many reports contain remarks from officials expressing surprise at how strongly freed people pursued education. One 1866 report from a Bureau officer in Virginia noted that formerly enslaved adults walked miles after labor hours to attend night classes.

The desire was not speculative.

It was written down.

THE RESISTANCE RECORDED IN OFFICIAL FILES

The same Bureau records also document opposition.

Agents filed reports describing school buildings burned, teachers threatened, and classes disrupted. These reports were not rumors. They were government communications sent to Washington and archived as official correspondence.

They list dates.

Locations.

Witnesses.

The pattern appears repeatedly across states.

Education was not simply encouraged or discouraged.

It was contested.

THE LAW STEPS IN

By the late nineteenth century, state legislatures across the South had enacted laws mandating racial segregation in public institutions, including schools. These statutes survive today in state legal codes and legislative archives.

The legal foundation for segregated schooling was reinforced by a decision still studied in constitutional law:

Plessy v. Ferguson (1896)

The ruling, preserved in United States Supreme Court Reports, upheld the doctrine of:

"separate but equal."

The phrase became a legal framework.

Not theory.

Policy.

On paper, the ruling required equality of facilities.

Archival education budgets from southern states in the early twentieth century, available in state financial reports and education board records, show that in practice, funding for schools serving Black students was often drastically lower than for white schools.

Historians did not invent this conclusion.

They calculated it from appropriations tables.

THE NUMBERS THAT TOLD THE STORY

State education reports from the early 1900s frequently itemize expenditures by district. When researchers analyze these documents, they often compare:

teacher salaries

school term length

building expenditures

textbook allocations

In multiple states, preserved records show disparities in each category.

Some school terms for Black students lasted only a few months per year, timed around agricultural labor seasons. The documentation appears in county school board minutes and superintendent reports.

The entries are routine.

The implications are not.

THE SCHOOLS BUILT DESPITE IT

Yet another set of records tells a parallel story.

Between 1912 and 1932, thousands of schools for Black children were constructed through a partnership between local communities and the Rosenwald Fund, a philanthropic program documented in detailed building reports preserved at Fisk University and the Library of Congress.

These records list:

school locations

construction costs

community contributions

student enrollment

Many entries note that local Black families donated land, labor, or materials when public funding was insufficient.

The documents reveal something often overlooked.

Communities documented their own progress when institutions would not.

THE COURTROOM RETURNS

By the mid-twentieth century, education records became central evidence in one of the most consequential legal decisions in American history.

Brown v. Board of Education (1954)

The case record, preserved in Supreme Court archives, included statistical studies, school district reports, and expert testimony demonstrating inequality between segregated schools.

The Court's unanimous ruling declared that segregated public education was inherently unequal.

The decision did not rely on rhetoric.

It relied on evidence.

Documents once created for administrative purposes became proof in a constitutional case.

THE ARCHIVE AS WITNESS

What makes the history of education after slavery so powerful is not merely what happened in classrooms. It is what was written about them.

Attendance ledgers.

Budget reports.

Inspection forms.

Construction records.

Each was created for routine administrative reasons.

Together, they formed a record of a national struggle over knowledge itself.

Because whoever shapes education shapes possibility.

WHAT HISTORIANS RECOGNIZE

Modern scholars consistently observe that systems of inequality rarely announce themselves openly. Instead, they appear in technical language, budgets, schedules, policies, zoning lines.

These documents rarely contain dramatic statements.

They contain numbers.

And numbers, when compared, tell stories that words sometimes hide. In the words of Jay-Z, men lie, women lie........ but numbers?.....

Chains once kept people from learning.

Later, learning itself became the contested ground.

And the evidence of that battle still sits quietly in archives.

END OF CHAPTER ANALYSIS

Enforcement, Authority, and the Visible Hand of Power

The evidence examined in this chapter illustrates how systems of authority become tangible through enforcement. Laws, policies, and administrative directives exist in written form, but their real-world impact depends on the mechanisms assigned to carry them out. Enforcement transforms instruction into action. Without it, statutes remain theory. With it, they become lived reality.

Institutional records consistently show that enforcement structures are rarely improvised. They are organized, delegated, and documented. Orders are issued. Reports are filed. Outcomes are recorded. This procedural chain allows authority to extend beyond the moment a rule is written. It ensures that policy does not remain abstract but operates within daily life.

From a legal perspective, enforcement is the point where law meets consequence. It is where authority becomes observable. Scholars studying administrative systems often focus on this stage because it reveals how rules function in practice rather than how they appear in theory. The documents preserved in the archive capture that interaction. They show how instructions were interpreted, how they were implemented, and what results followed.

Such records demonstrate that enforcement is not merely an accessory to governance. It is one of its defining instruments.

LEGAL REFLECTION

A rule written is authority declared.

A rule enforced is authority realized.

The difference between the two is the difference between policy and power.

FINAL TRANSITION

The materials referenced in this chapter survive in official repositories, preserved alongside the directives that produced them. They form a documentary trail that allows later readers to examine how authority was exercised in real time.

Those documents remain accessible.

The order was issued.

The record shows it was carried out.......

PRIMARY SOURCE DOSSIER — VERIFIED RECORDS

Readers can independently research:

Freedmen's Bureau Education Reports — National Archives RG 105

State legislative segregation statutes — state archives (1870–1950)

Plessy v. Ferguson (1896) — U.S. Supreme Court Reports

State education budgets — early 20th-century legislative records

Rosenwald School Building Reports — Fisk University / Library of Congress

Brown v. Board of Education (1954) — Supreme Court case archive

Chapter Eight

Chapter 8 THE MAPS THAT DIVIDED CITIES

Lines Drawn in Ink That Became Walls in Real Life

The lines looked harmless......

Thin. Precise.

Carefully drawn across paper maps.

No barbed wire.

No guards.

No gates.

Just ink.....

Yet those lines would decide where people could live, where they could borrow money, where they could build wealth, and where opportunity would stop.

Because sometimes power does not build walls.

It draws them.

THE MAP ROOM

In the 1930s, government agencies across the United States began producing detailed residential maps of major cities. These maps still exist today in digitized form through the Mapping Inequality Project, which compiles original federal housing documents from the National Archives.

At first glance, they appear technical, color-coded city plans marked with letters and shading. Neighborhoods were graded according to perceived lending risk.

Green.

Blue.

Yellow.

Red.

The colors were not decorative.

They were instructions.

THE GRADING SYSTEM

The maps were produced as part of programs administered by the Home Owners' Loan Corporation (HOLC), a federal entity created in 1933. Field agents surveyed neighborhoods and wrote area descriptions that were attached to each map.

These assessment sheets survive. They are preserved in federal archives and university collections.

They evaluated neighborhoods using categories such as:

housing condition

income level

infrastructure

population composition

It is the last category that historians most often study closely.

Because in many preserved area descriptions, the racial or ethnic makeup of residents is explicitly mentioned as a factor influencing the neighborhood's grade.

The documents do not disguise this language.

They record it.

THE COLOR RED

Neighborhoods outlined in red were labeled as the highest lending risk.

The term commonly used in the documents,

"Hazardous."

Banks reviewing these maps often treated the grading as guidance for mortgage decisions. Researchers comparing lending data with these maps have documented patterns showing that areas marked in red frequently received fewer approved loans.

The practice later became widely known as,

"Redlining".

The word was not invented later.

It came from the color on the maps.

WHAT THE FILES ACTUALLY SAY

The original neighborhood evaluation forms contain typed descriptions written by field agents. These forms are among the most striking archival materials historians encounter because they are candid administrative assessments, not public statements.

They include remarks about,

property values,

neighborhood stability,

And perceived desirability.

Many also contain demographic observations written in plain language.

The significance lies not in interpretation, but in existence. These assessments were created as official documents and stored as such. They were not hidden memoranda. They were part of routine federal housing analysis.

WHEN A MAP BECOMES POLICY

A map alone does nothing.

But when institutions use it, the map becomes a decision-making tool.

Scholars who study twentieth-century housing policy often compare:

HOLC maps

Federal Housing Administration loan records

And city planning documents.

When layered together, these sources reveal patterns in how credit and development flowed through cities.

Some areas saw rapid mortgage growth.

Others saw almost none.

The documents do not always explain why.

They show where.

THE ARCHIVE OF ABSENCE

One of the most powerful forms of historical evidence is absence, the absence of investment, loans, or infrastructure in particular areas over long periods. (Is the evidence of absence, the absence of evidence? -Gin Rummy.

Historians analyzing municipal records, property assessments, and lending statistics often find decades where some neighborhoods show minimal institutional investment.

Not because nothing happened.

Because nothing was approved.

That absence leaves a trail in,

bank reports,

municipal budgets,

census tract data,

And real estate records.

When viewed individually, each document appears technical.

Together, they form a pattern.

THE COURTROOM RETURNS AGAIN

Housing documentation eventually entered the legal arena. In the mid-twentieth century, court cases challenged discriminatory housing practices using evidence drawn directly from real estate contracts and lending files.

One of the most significant:

Shelley v. Kraemer (1948)

This Supreme Court decision addressed racially restrictive housing covenants, clauses in property deeds that limited who could buy or occupy land. Copies of such covenants survive in county deed records across the United States.

The Court ruled that courts could not enforce these restrictions.

The ruling did not erase the documents.

It prevented their enforcement.

And so the covenants remain preserved today in property archives, historical evidence of how ownership had once been restricted.

WHAT HISTORIANS SEE IN THE MAPS

Modern researchers often compare historical redlining maps with present-day demographic and economic data. These comparisons, published in peer-reviewed studies, frequently show correlations between past grading classifications and later patterns of:

property values

infrastructure investment

public health outcomes

environmental conditions

The conclusion is not drawn from speculation.

It is drawn from layered records.

Maps from one decade.

Statistics from another.

Policies from another.

Each document alone is limited.

Together, they become explanatory.

THE QUIET POWER OF CARTOGRAPHY

Maps are persuasive because they appear neutral. Lines look mathematical. Colors look objective. But historians of cartography emphasize that every map reflects the priorities of the people who created it.

A map does not simply show reality.

It selects it.

And when institutions rely on those selections, the map shapes outcomes in the real world.

Some barriers are built from brick.

Others are drawn in ink.

The brick can crumble.

The ink can last centuries.

END OF CHAPTER ANALYSIS

Surveillance, Documentation, and the Administrative Gaze

The materials examined in this chapter demonstrate that authority is not exercised only through action. It is also exercised through observation. Systems that monitor, record, and report are capable of influencing behavior even before any directive is issued. Surveillance, in its administrative sense, is not merely watching; it is documenting what is seen and preserving it within institutional memory.

Documentation transforms observation into authority. A moment witnessed may pass. A moment recorded can be referenced, evaluated, and acted upon. This is why bureaucratic systems historically placed such emphasis on reports, registries, logs, and summaries. They were tools that converted information into usable data. Once entered into official records, information could travel through administrative channels, shaping decisions far removed from the original event.

Legal scholars often note that the power of documentation lies in its permanence. An observation spoken may be disputed. An observation written becomes part of the file. Files accumulate, and accumulated files form the basis of institutional knowledge. The records explored in this chapter illustrate how systems used documentation not only to respond to events, but to anticipate and manage them.

Such practices reveal that surveillance, when formalized through recordkeeping, becomes a mechanism of governance rather than a mere act of watching.

LEGAL REFLECTION

Observation sees.

Documentation remembers.

And what is remembered can be used.

FINAL TRANSITION

The reports, logs, and registries discussed in this chapter remain preserved in archival collections, organized according to the administrative systems that created them. They stand as written evidence of how observation became record and how record became authority.

They can still be examined.

They watched.

They wrote it down.

The record endured......

PRIMARY SOURCE DOSSIER — VERIFIED ARCHIVES

Readers can independently consult:

Home Owners' Loan Corporation Residential Security Maps — National Archives / Mapping Inequality Project

HOLC Area Description Forms — federal archival collections

Federal Housing Administration lending manuals — National Archives

Property deed records with restrictive covenants — county registries

Shelley v. Kraemer (1948) — U.S. Supreme Court Reports

Chapter 9
THE FILES OF SURVEILLANCE

When Watching Became Policy

The watchers rarely appeared in photographs.

They did not stand in crowds.

They did not march.

They did not speak.

They wrote.

Because surveillance, in its most powerful form, does not operate through noise.

It operates through files.

THE CABINETS THAT HELD LIVES

In government buildings across the United States during the twentieth century, rows of metal filing cabinets stored folders stamped with dates, numbers, and classification codes. Many of these folders are now declassified and preserved in federal archives.

Inside them are reports.

Not rumors.

Not legends.

Reports.

Typed summaries.

Observation notes.

Transcripts.

Memoranda.

They describe meetings attended, speeches given, letters sent, travel routes taken, organizations joined.

These documents were not written decades later.

They were written in real time.

THE PROGRAM THAT LEFT A PAPER TRAIL

Among the most extensively documented surveillance operations in U.S. history is one formally known as:

COINTELPRO

(Counter Intelligence Program)

This program, conducted by the Federal Bureau of Investigation between 1956 and 1971, is not speculative. It is confirmed through thousands of pages of declassified files released under the Freedom of Information Act and congressional investigations.

The FBI's own internal memoranda, now publicly accessible, state that the program targeted groups considered politically subversive. These files include directives, field reports, and internal evaluations.

The significance lies not in allegation.

It lies in documentation written by the agency itself.

THE MEMORANDUM THAT HISTORIANS QUOTE

One of the most cited internal documents from the program is a directive written in 1967 outlining objectives for monitoring certain political movements. The memo is preserved in FBI records and was later reproduced in the findings of the U.S. Senate Select Committee to Study Governmental Operations, commonly known as the Church Committee (1975–1976).

That committee's published report concluded that intelligence agencies had engaged in surveillance activities that raised serious constitutional concerns.

The report is publicly available.

Bound. Indexed. Archived.

HOW SURVEILLANCE WAS DOCUMENTED

The surviving files reveal a methodical structure. Field offices submitted periodic updates that included:

names of attendees at meetings

summaries of speeches

travel logs

copies of correspondence

photographs

Each entry followed a format.

Date.

Location.

Subject.

Observation.

Historians examining these documents often note how routine they appear. The tone is administrative, not dramatic. The agents who wrote them were filing reports, not composing narratives.

Yet those reports now function as historical evidence.

THE POWER OF A FILE NUMBER

One of the most striking features of surveillance archives is the numerical system attached to each file. Individuals and organizations were assigned identification numbers used across multiple documents.

To the agency, these numbers allowed efficient record-keeping.

To historians, they provide something else:

Continuity.

A single file number can connect dozens of documents spanning years, revealing patterns of observation that no single report would show alone.

In other words:

The file becomes a timeline.

WHEN DOCUMENTS BECAME PUBLIC

Much of what is known today about domestic surveillance programs comes from official investigations conducted in the 1970s. The Church Committee hearings, preserved in congressional records, examined intelligence activities carried out by federal agencies.

The committee's final reports documented instances of surveillance conducted without judicial oversight. These findings did not rely on speculation; they relied on agency files reviewed by investigators.

The reports themselves are now historical documents.

They testify not only to surveillance—but to the investigation of surveillance.

WHAT HISTORIANS NOTICE FIRST

When scholars first encounter these declassified records, many describe a similar reaction: surprise at the level of detail preserved.

Not because surveillance existed, that is well known in modern states, but because the documentation is so thorough.

Some files contain

minute-by-minute event descriptions,

physical location diagrams,

Or verbatim quotations.

The completeness of these records means historians do not have to guess how monitoring worked.

They can read it.

THE ARCHIVE'S DOUBLE ROLE

Surveillance files occupy a unique place in historical research because they serve two functions simultaneously:

They are records of observation.

And they are artifacts of power.

Every report reveals not only information about the subject being observed, but also the priorities of the institution doing the observing.

What an agency chooses to document tells historians what it considered important.

And what it considered important reveals what it feared.

THE SILENCE BETWEEN REPORTS

Equally revealing are the gaps.

Periods where documentation suddenly stops.

Names that disappear from files.

Investigations that end without explanation.

Archivists often note that silence in a record can be as meaningful as its contents. It can indicate a shift in policy, priorities, or authority.

Absence, when recorded, becomes evidence.

Walls confine the body.

But files can follow a person anywhere.

And once written, they can outlive everyone involved.......

END OF CHAPTER ANALYSIS

Bodies, Records, and the Authority of Measurement

The documents explored in this chapter reveal how institutions convert the human body into measurable data. Measurement appears neutral. Numbers appear objective. Yet the act of measuring is never entirely passive. It reflects what a system considers important enough to quantify.

Administrative structures depend on metrics because metrics allow comparison, allocation, and regulation. Once recorded, measurements can influence funding decisions, policy priorities, and institutional responses. The archive shows that when bodies become entries in official records, those entries can travel far beyond the original context in which they were created.

Legal systems often rely on documented measurement when evaluating claims. Statistics may be cited in court opinions, legislative debates, and administrative reviews. The authority of numbers can shape interpretation as powerfully as eyewitness testimony. For that reason, the creation and preservation of quantitative records become acts of governance in themselves.

The chapter's materials demonstrate that measurement does not merely describe reality. It participates in shaping it. When bodies are recorded as data, the data can inform policy. When policy is informed by data, outcomes follow.

LEGAL REFLECTION

To measure is to define.

To define is to influence.

What is counted becomes visible.

What is visible can be governed.

FINAL TRANSITION

The statistical tables, reports, and institutional records referenced here remain archived in national repositories and government collections. They stand as preserved evidence of how measurement entered administrative systems and how those systems relied upon it.

They remain open to examination.

They reduced the body to numbers.

The numbers shaped the system.

PRIMARY SOURCE DOSSIER — VERIFIED ARCHIVES

Readers can independently consult:

FBI COINTELPRO files — released via Freedom of Information Act

Church Committee Reports (1976) — U.S. Senate archives

Declassified intelligence memoranda — National Archives collections

Congressional intelligence oversight reports — Library of Congress

FBI Records: The Vault — public digital archive maintained by the Federal Bureau of Investigation

Chapter Ten

Chapter 10 THE LEDGERS OF INEQUALITY

When Wealth Was Calculated Before It Was Earned

Money rarely announces its rules.

It does not shout them.

It does not post them on courthouse doors.

It records them.

Quietly.

In ledgers.

Because long before a person ever applies for a loan, signs a mortgage, or opens an account, numbers have already begun deciding what will be possible.

And numbers, once written, tend to stay written.

THE ROOMS WHERE DECISIONS WERE TALLIED

In banks across the twentieth century, clerks filled out forms that determined whether a borrower was approved or denied. These forms, many preserved today in federal banking archives and historical lending collections, look technical and routine.

Boxes.

Codes.

Ratings.

Signatures.

They resemble nothing dramatic.

Yet historians studying financial archives often emphasize that these documents functioned as gatekeepers. They determined who could obtain capital, who could buy property, who could build businesses, and who could not.

Because modern economies run not only on currency.

They run on approval.

THE INVENTION OF CREDIT FILES

By the early twentieth century, private credit bureaus had begun compiling detailed financial reports on individuals. Surviving records from early credit reporting agencies, preserved in business archives and regulatory filings, show how these systems operated.

Reports often included:

employment history

payment history

debts

personal reputation notes

Some early twentieth-century credit reports even contained subjective remarks written by investigators who interviewed neighbors or employers. Historians examining such documents note that these remarks could influence whether a loan was granted.

The reports were not rumors.

They were official business records.

THE FEDERAL GUIDELINES

During the 1930s and 1940s, federal agencies issued lending manuals to guide mortgage decisions. One widely studied example is the Federal Housing Administration underwriting manual, preserved in National Archives collections.

These manuals instructed lenders how to evaluate risk when issuing home loans. They contained technical language about property values, neighborhood stability, and long-term investment security.

Researchers who analyze these manuals often focus on how they linked lending decisions to neighborhood characteristics. The language appears procedural. Yet its implications affected access to homeownership for decades.

The manual did not decide loans itself.

It shaped how loans were decided.

THE POWER OF APPROVAL

Economic historians frequently point out that access to credit has historically been one of the strongest predictors of wealth accumulation. This conclusion comes not from theory but from decades of financial data preserved in banking reports, census tables, and housing statistics.

When researchers compare:

loan approval rates

property ownership records

long-term asset growth

they often find strong relationships between credit access and financial stability across generations.

These findings appear in peer-reviewed studies using archival datasets.

The pattern is not anecdotal.

It is statistical.

THE FILE THAT FOLLOWED YOU

Unlike a single transaction, a financial file grows over time. Each payment, missed payment, loan, or inquiry becomes another entry.

Modern credit reporting systems, regulated today under federal law such as the Fair Credit Reporting Act (1970), require documentation standards for maintaining and correcting such records. The law itself is preserved in the United States Statutes at Large and congressional archives.

What historians note about financial files is their persistence. A record created years earlier can influence decisions years later.

Not because someone remembers it.

Because the file does.

THE DATA THAT RESEARCHERS COMPARE

Scholars analyzing long-term economic inequality often rely on historical datasets compiled from government statistical reports, including those published by:

the U.S. Census Bureau

the Federal Reserve

the Department of Commerce

These reports provide numerical snapshots of income, assets, and lending patterns across different decades.

Individually, each report is just a table.

Together, they become a timeline.

And timelines reveal trajectories.

WHEN NUMBERS REPLACE WORDS

One of the most striking features of financial documentation is its neutrality of tone. Ledgers do not accuse. They do not justify. They do not narrate.

They calculate.

This neutrality can make financial records appear objective, yet historians emphasize that numbers always reflect the systems that generate them. What is measured, how it is measured, and what is ignored all shape the final figure.

The ledger is silent.

But its totals speak.

THE ARCHIVE AS ECONOMIC MEMORY

Physical wealth can be lost. Buildings collapse. Businesses fail. Markets fluctuate.

But financial records preserve something else: the history of decisions.

Loan approved.

Loan denied.

Interest rate assigned.

Collateral required.

Each entry is a moment where possibility either opened or closed.

Multiply those moments across millions of people and decades of time, and the ledger becomes more than accounting.

It becomes history written in currency.

A chain can restrict movement.

A number can restrict opportunity.

And numbers, once entered into the record, can travel farther than any chain ever could.

END OF CHAPTER ANALYSIS

Mortality, Documentation, and the Record of Loss

The materials examined in this chapter reveal how institutions record death. Mortality is not only a human event; it is an administrative one. When a life ends, a certificate is issued, a cause is entered, a file is opened, and an official record is created. That record becomes part of the statistical fabric through which societies understand themselves.

Documentation of death serves multiple purposes. It confirms identity, establishes legal closure, and contributes to demographic analysis. Yet it also reflects institutional priorities. The way causes are categorized, the language used, and the consistency of reporting can shape how patterns are interpreted by later researchers.

Legal systems treat mortality records as authoritative. Courts rely on death certificates. Legislatures consult mortality data when shaping public policy. Scholars use statistical summaries to analyze trends. Because of this, the initial entry of a cause of death carries weight beyond the moment of its creation.

The chapter's evidence demonstrates that mortality documentation does more than record individual loss. It aggregates into patterns that influence institutional response. What is listed becomes counted. What is counted becomes analyzed. What is analyzed can inform decisions.

Thus, the archive of death is also an archive of governance.

LEGAL REFLECTION

A life ends once.

The record of it remains.

What is written on the certificate can echo through policy long after the burial.

FINAL TRANSITION

The coroner reports, certificates, and statistical summaries discussed in this chapter remain preserved in public archives, health departments, and national repositories. They exist not as narrative, but as official documentation—entries made at specific moments in time by authorized offices.

They can still be reviewed.

The burial was brief.

The record was permanent.

PRIMARY SOURCE DOSSIER — VERIFIED ARCHIVAL SOURCES

Readers may consult:

Federal Housing Administration Underwriting Manuals — National Archives

Early credit bureau records — business history archives

Fair Credit Reporting Act (1970) — U.S. Statutes at Large

Federal Reserve historical wealth data reports

U.S. Census economic statistics series

Department of Commerce financial reports

Chapter Eleven

Chapter 11 THE FILES OF HEALTH AND SURVIVAL

When Life Expectancy Was Recorded in Columns

Hospitals are designed to heal.

White walls.

Clean sheets.

Sterile instruments.

Everything about them suggests protection.

Yet in archives across the United States exist medical records, administrative reports, and public health documents showing that access to care, like housing, education, and credit, was not always distributed equally.

Not by rumor.

By record.

THE LEDGERS OF ADMISSION

Early twentieth-century hospital admission books, preserved in medical school archives and state historical collections, often list patients in neat rows by

Name.

Age.

Condition.

Outcome.

Some also contain another column.

Race.

These ledgers were administrative tools, not political statements. Clerks recorded information required for reporting and budgeting. But for historians studying public health history, those entries provide measurable evidence of how medical treatment systems were structured.

Because once something is written down consistently, it can be studied.

SEGREGATED WARDS, DOCUMENTED

Throughout the late nineteenth and early twentieth centuries, many hospitals in the United States operated segregated facilities. Evidence for this is not anecdotal; it appears in:

- hospital policy manuals
- architectural plans
- state health department inspections
- funding reports

Some inspection reports preserved in state archives list ward assignments by race when evaluating facility capacity. The tone of these documents is technical, not emotional. They discuss bed counts, sanitation, and staffing ratios.

Yet between the lines, historians see a pattern:

Medical care was being administered inside a divided system.

THE REPORTS THAT MEASURED HEALTH

Public health agencies have long collected statistical data. Annual reports from state health departments and federal agencies, many now digitized, contain tables tracking:

- mortality rates
- disease incidence
- life expectancy

Researchers comparing these tables across decades often analyze disparities between populations. Because the data was collected consistently, it allows long-term comparisons.

Numbers do not argue.

They accumulate.

THE STUDY THAT BECAME A RECORD

One of the most widely studied medical research archives in American history is the documentation of the **Tuskegee Syphilis Study (1932–1972)**. The surviving records include government correspondence, research notes, and participant logs preserved in the National Archives.

The study, conducted by the U.S. Public Health Service, tracked hundreds of participants over decades. In 1972, public reporting brought national attention to the study's procedures, prompting congressional hearings and official investigations.

Those hearings produced transcripts.

Those transcripts became records.

And those records remain accessible today.

WHEN INVESTIGATION CREATES EVIDENCE

Following the public exposure of the study, federal inquiries examined its conduct. Reports from these investigations, held in congressional archives, document the findings of oversight bodies reviewing the program.

The significance of these materials lies in their origin:

They were produced by the same governmental system that conducted the inquiry.

Not outside accusation.

Inside review.

This is one of the most powerful forms of historical documentation: institutional self-examination.

THE STATISTICS THAT FOLLOWED

Public health researchers today often use historical datasets compiled by agencies such as the Centers for Disease Control and the National Center for Health Statistics. These databases combine decades of recorded information into long-range statistical timelines.

By analyzing these datasets, scholars can observe changes in life expectancy, disease prevalence, and access to care over time.

The conclusions drawn from such research do not rely on memory.

They rely on measurement.

WHAT HISTORIANS OF MEDICINE NOTE

Medical historians consistently observe that healthcare systems mirror the social structures in which they exist. When society changes, medical access patterns often change with it.

The archives show this progression.

Earlier reports.

Later reports.

Comparisons between them.

The pattern emerges not because someone declared it, but because the numbers align.

THE QUIET AUTHORITY OF DATA

A testimony can be disputed.

An opinion can be challenged.

But a dataset compiled year after year, across decades, acquires a different kind of authority. Its power comes from continuity.

The longer a record is kept, the more it reveals.

Because trends do not appear in a single entry.

They appear across time.

A person's life can be measured in years.

But history measures systems by what those years look like.

And the record keeps both.

END OF CHAPTER ANALYSIS

Data, Policy, and the Quiet Architecture of Decision

The documents examined in this chapter reveal how aggregated data becomes the foundation of institutional policy. Individual records, once collected and compiled, form statistical portraits. Those portraits influence funding, enforcement priorities, legislative proposals, and administrative reform.

Data carries authority because it appears impartial. Tables and charts suggest objectivity. Yet every dataset reflects a prior decision about what to measure, how to categorize, and how to interpret results. The archive shows that before numbers shape policy, someone chooses what counts.

Legal and administrative systems routinely rely on statistical evidence. Courts cite demographic data. Legislatures consult population reports. Agencies justify actions through quantified findings. Once entered into official publications, statistics acquire institutional force. They move beyond observation and into governance.

This chapter demonstrates that data does not merely describe systems, it helps steer them. When policymakers act based on compiled records, the archive becomes an instrument of direction.

LEGAL REFLECTION

Numbers appear neutral.

Policies rarely are.

What is measured influences what is decided.

FINAL TRANSITION

The reports, statistical abstracts, and government publications referenced here remain housed in national archives, research libraries, and official repositories. They are preserved as formal publications, not interpretations, but data as recorded by institutions themselves.

They remain open to scrutiny.

The numbers were printed.

The policies followed.

PRIMARY SOURCE DOSSIER VERIFIED ARCHIVES

Readers may consult:

• Historic hospital admission ledgers — medical university archives

• State health department annual reports — state archives

• U.S. Public Health Service study records — National Archives

• Congressional hearing transcripts (1970s investigations) — U.S. Government Publishing Office

• National Center for Health Statistics datasets — federal databases

Chapter Twelve

Chapter 12
THE FILES OF CONTROL OVER THE BODY

When Authority Extended Beneath the Skin

The body seems like the one thing a person owns completely.

It travels where you go.

It bears your scars.

It carries your voice.

It is the only possession that cannot be separated from you.

At least, that is how it feels.

But in the archives of courts, hospitals, and legislatures are records showing that control over the human body has often been debated, defined, limited, and reassigned, not symbolically, but legally.

Because once authority is written into law, it can reach further than any hand ever could.

WHEN LAW DEFINES THE BODY

Legal historians frequently emphasize that one of the most powerful questions any legal system answers is this:

Who has authority over a person's body?

Court transcripts preserved in judicial archives show that this question has appeared repeatedly in different forms across American history. Sometimes it arose in criminal cases. Sometimes in medical rulings. Sometimes in constitutional disputes.

Each time, the answer was not philosophical.

It was recorded.

THE CASE FILES OF FORCED DECISION

Among the most studied twentieth-century legal cases involving bodily autonomy is,

Buck v. Bell (1927)

The decision, preserved in the official United States Supreme Court Reports, addressed a Virginia statute allowing compulsory sterilization of certain individuals classified by the state as unfit.

The Court upheld the law.

The ruling did not speculate. It issued a written opinion. That opinion remains publicly accessible in the national legal archive.

Historians studying public health law often analyze this case because it demonstrates how medical procedures, when authorized by statute, can become matters of legal policy rather than individual choice.

The significance is not rumor.

It is precedent.

THE RECORDS OF IMPLEMENTATION

State institutional reports from the early twentieth century, held in state archives and university special collections, contain administrative logs documenting sterilization procedures performed under such laws.

These records typically list,

date

institution

authorization number

physician

patient classification

They read like hospital paperwork.

Which is precisely what they were.

Clerks filled them out as part of routine reporting requirements. Yet historians examining these files note that routine paperwork often becomes the clearest historical evidence of how a policy functioned in practice.

Because policies can be debated.

Records show what happened.

THE INVESTIGATIONS THAT FOLLOWED

Decades later, legislative inquiries and academic studies began reviewing historical sterilization programs. Some states commissioned official reports examining archival institutional data to understand how widely such policies had been implemented.

These reports, many publicly released, were compiled from original documents such as patient files, administrative correspondence, and hospital records.

They did not reconstruct events from memory.

They read them from files.

THE LANGUAGE OF AUTHORIZATION

One of the most striking features of institutional records from this period is the vocabulary they use. Words like:

authorized

approved

certified

recommended

appear repeatedly in administrative documents.

The tone is clinical.

Detached.

Procedural.

Historians often observe that bureaucratic language has a unique effect: it can transform actions that would otherwise appear dramatic into routine entries in a file.

Not because the events were small.

Because the language was standardized.

WHEN POLICY BECOMES PRECEDENT

Legal decisions rarely remain isolated. Once a ruling is issued, it becomes part of a larger body of law. Future courts may cite it, interpret it, or limit it, but they must acknowledge it.

This is why case law archives matter so deeply to historians and legal scholars. They show how authority evolves over time.

A ruling from one decade

appears again in arguments decades later.

The original decision becomes a reference point.

And reference points shape outcomes.

THE ARCHIVE AS A MEDICAL HISTORY

Medical records, institutional files, and legal decisions together form a layered historical archive. No single document explains everything. But when researchers compare them, patterns can emerge.

A statute authorizes a practice.

A hospital implements it.

A court reviews it.

A report analyzes it.

Each layer produces paperwork.

And paperwork accumulates.

WHAT RESEARCHERS SEE WHEN THEY COMPARE FILES

Modern scholars studying historical medical policy often combine multiple sources:

court rulings

hospital records

legislative statutes

statistical reports

When placed side by side, these materials reveal how legal authority, medical practice, and administrative procedure interacted.

Not abstractly.

Operationally.

The system becomes visible only when its documents are viewed together.

WHY THESE RECORDS MATTER

The significance of these archives is not limited to what they describe. It lies in what they demonstrate,

Authority can be exercised through procedure.

Not loudly.

Not violently.

Formally.

Stamped.

Filed.

Signed.

And once a decision is recorded in official form, it gains a kind of durability that memory alone cannot match.

Force can restrain the body for a moment.
Law can restrain it for generations.
And the archive remembers which one was used.

END OF CHAPTER ANALYSIS

The Body as File, The File as Authority

The materials examined in this chapter reveal a recurring institutional pattern: when the body enters administrative systems, it becomes documentation. Medical reports, institutional logs, confinement records, intake forms, and treatment summaries convert lived physical experience into official entries.

These records do more than describe conditions. They authorize action.

In legal systems, written documentation of bodily status can determine custody, confinement, treatment, release, or restriction. Once a condition is entered into a file, it becomes part of a chain of decisions. Subsequent administrators rely on prior entries. Each record builds upon the last.

Institutional archives show that documentation of the body has historically served as both description and justification. Reports were written not only to record events, but to legitimize administrative outcomes. A written evaluation could shape years of institutional response.

From a legal perspective, bodily documentation carries particular weight because it intersects with questions of autonomy, consent, and authority. Courts often treat official records as presumptively reliable unless challenged. As a result, the initial recording of information can have enduring consequences.

This chapter demonstrates that once the body becomes part of the file, it enters the jurisdiction of the institution.

LEGAL REFLECTION

The body was examined.

The report was written.

The decision followed.

In systems of administration, documentation can outlive the moment it describes.

FINAL TRANSITION

The medical records, institutional logs, and administrative summaries referenced in this chapter remain preserved in archival collections and official repositories. They stand not as retrospective interpretations, but as contemporaneous documentation created by authorized personnel.

They can still be accessed and examined.

The body healed or did not.

The file remained.

PRIMARY SOURCE DOSSIER — VERIFIED ARCHIVAL RECORDS

Readers may consult:

Buck v. Bell (1927) — United States Supreme Court Reports

State sterilization program records — state archives and university collections

Legislative investigative reports on sterilization policies — state government publications

Institutional medical reports (early 20th century) — historical medical archives

Congressional hearings on medical ethics — U.S. Government Publishing Office

Chapter Thirteen

Chapter 13 THE FILES OF VIOLENCE WITHOUT CONSEQUENCE

When the Record Shows the Crime but Not the Punishment

The document exists...

That is the first thing investigators notice when they open the file.

Not rumor.

Not legend.

A report.

Typed. Dated. Signed.

It states that something happened.

An assault.

A killing.

A disappearance.

The event is recorded.

And yet,

No conviction follows.

THE ARCHIVE OF UNFINISHED CASES

In county courthouses, state archives, and federal repositories across the United States are preserved thousands of criminal case files from the late nineteenth and early twentieth centuries. Many are thin folders containing only a few few pages:

Complaint.

Statement.

Witness name.

Disposition.

Historians who study these records often point out that the most revealing entry is the last line.

Because sometimes it reads, Case closed. With no verdict attached.

THE INVESTIGATIVE REPORTS THAT REMAIN

One of the most important bodies of documentation concerning unresolved acts of racial violence is preserved in federal records generated decades after the events themselves. In the early 2000s, the U.S. government initiated formal reviews of historical civil rights–era cases through what became known as the Cold Case Initiative of the U.S. Department of Justice.

Investigators examined archived files from earlier decades, including:

FBI reports

local police records

Showed coroner statements

witness interviews

These were not newly invented allegations. They were historical files that had existed for years, sometimes decades, before being re-opened.

The significance lies in their origin:

The evidence had always been there.

THE CONGRESSIONAL RECORD

In 2008, Congress passed legislation directing federal authorities to review unresolved civil rights–era homicide cases. The statute, preserved in federal legislative archives, required examination of historical investigative files to determine whether further legal action was possible.

The law itself is public record.

So are the reports produced under it.

These reports contain summaries of evidence gathered long ago, often showing that investigations had once begun but did not proceed to prosecution.

The documents do not speculate.

They list findings.

THE PATTERN HISTORIANS IDENTIFY

When researchers compare multiple historical criminal files from the Reconstruction era through the mid-twentieth century, they sometimes observe a recurring structure:

Incident recorded.

Witness statements taken.

Suspect named.

Proceedings halted.

The reason for halting varies. Sometimes it is listed as:

insufficient evidence

unavailable witnesses

jurisdictional limitations

Each explanation appears procedural.

And procedure, when written down, appears legitimate.

That is why historians rely on records, not impressions, to understand what occurred.

THE TESTIMONY PRESERVED IN PRINT

During the late nineteenth century, congressional committees investigated violence in parts of the South. Transcripts of these hearings, preserved today in the Library of Congress and federal archives, contain sworn testimony from witnesses describing attacks, intimidation, and threats.

The transcripts are lengthy. Detailed. Formal.

They include:

questions

answers

dates

names

Nothing about them is dramatic in tone.

They read like stenographic records.

Which is exactly what they are.

Their power lies in their format, sworn testimony entered into official government proceedings.

WHEN THE RECORD OUTLIVES THE MOMENT

Violence can be immediate.

Records are permanent.

A crime may last minutes.

A report about it can last centuries.

Historians often emphasize that documentation changes the nature of historical evidence. An event without a record can be debated.

An event with a record must be interpreted, but it cannot be dismissed as easily.

Because a document is not memory.

It is proof that someone, at a specific time, wrote down what they believed had occurred.

THE ROLE OF THE CLERK, AGAIN

As in earlier chapters, one figure appears repeatedly in these histories:

The clerk.

Not the detective.

Not the judge.

Not the prosecutor.

The clerk.

The clerk logs the complaint. Files the testimony. Records the disposition. Stamps the date. Moves to the next case.

Clerks rarely intended to preserve history.

Yet without them, much of history would not be preserved at all.

THE DIFFERENCE BETWEEN LAW AND OUTCOME

Legal historians often distinguish between two separate realities:

What the law says.

What the system does.

Criminal statutes may prohibit violence. Court procedures may outline prosecution. But case files show that enforcement is a process, not a guarantee.

The archive reveals this distinction clearly.

Because the law is written in codes.

The outcome is written in files.

WHAT MODERN RESEARCHERS FIND

Scholars reviewing historical criminal justice records frequently rely on multi-source comparisons:

court dockets

newspaper reports

coroner logs

police files

Individually, each source offers a fragment. Together, they allow reconstruction of events and responses.

Patterns sometimes emerge not from a single dramatic case, but from repetition across many ordinary ones.

That is how systems become visible:

Through accumulation.

THE QUIET POWER OF DOCUMENTED SILENCE

Silence in a record can be as meaningful as testimony.

A missing verdict.

An unsigned warrant.

An unfiled charge.

Archivists often note that gaps are not empty. They are data. They show where something expected did not occur.

And when absence appears repeatedly across records, it becomes historically significant.

Violence can disappear from sight.

But once written into a file, it never fully disappears from history.

END OF CHAPTER ANALYSIS

Economics, Contracts, and the Paperwork of Obligation

The records examined in this chapter reveal how economic systems are sustained through documentation. Contracts, wage agreements, debt ledgers, share arrangements, and financial correspondence transform labor and obligation into enforceable instruments. Once signed and recorded, agreements acquire legal weight.

Economic authority does not operate through force alone. It operates through obligation formalized on paper. A contract establishes terms. A ledger tracks compliance. A receipt confirms payment or deficiency. Together, these documents create a structure within which economic relationships are defined and regulated.

From a legal standpoint, contracts are among the most powerful tools of governance. Courts enforce them. Statutes define their validity. Institutions rely upon them to allocate responsibility and resolve disputes. When economic systems are documented, they become subject to procedural review, but they also gain institutional protection.

The archive demonstrates that financial records rarely stand in isolation. They interact with legal codes, administrative oversight, and enforcement mechanisms. Debt entries can lead to court actions. Contract disputes can trigger litigation. Economic documentation thus becomes a bridge between private transaction and public authority.

This chapter shows that obligation, once recorded, becomes part of a larger administrative system. The document is not merely proof of agreement; it is an instrument of enforcement.

LEGAL REFLECTION

A promise spoken can fade.

A promise written can bind.

Once entered into the ledger, obligation gains force.

FINAL TRANSITION

The contracts, ledgers, and economic records discussed here remain preserved in archives, special collections, and institutional repositories. They are artifacts of transaction, tangible evidence of how economic systems were structured and administered.

They remain open to examination.

The ink dried on the agreement.

The obligation endured……

PRIMARY SOURCE DOSSIER — VERIFIED ARCHIVES

Readers may consult:

U.S. Department of Justice Cold Case Initiative reports — federal archives

Congressional investigation transcripts (19th–20th century) — Library of Congress

Reconstruction-era criminal case dockets — state archives

FBI civil rights–era investigative files — National Archives

Coroner and inquest records — county historical collections

Chapter Fourteen

Chapter 14 When a Line on a Form Determined a Life

Before a person could vote, work, travel, own property, marry, or be counted, they had to be classified.

Not socially.

Officially.

Because governments do not interact with individuals as personalities. They interact with them as entries.

Entries on forms.

Entries in ledgers.

Entries in census rolls.

And once a category is written beside a name, that category can begin to shape everything that follows.

THE FIRST NATIONAL LIST

In 1790, the United States conducted its first federal census. The schedules from that enumeration, preserved in the National Archives, contain columns dividing inhabitants into legally recognized classifications.

The categories were not neutral descriptions.

They were legal distinctions.

Early census forms separated populations into columns such as:

- free persons
- enslaved persons
- other persons

Each classification had consequences. Representation in Congress, taxation formulas, and political power calculations depended on those numbers. The census was not just a count.

It was a structure.

WHEN CLASSIFICATION BECOMES LAW

Throughout the nineteenth and early twentieth centuries, state statutes and court decisions increasingly defined how individuals would be classified racially in legal documents.

One of the most frequently cited examples preserved in court records is:

Plessy v. Ferguson (1896)

While widely known for its ruling on segregation, the case itself also depended on legal classification. Court transcripts show that arguments hinged on whether Homer Plessy could legally be categorized under state racial statutes.

The law did not ask how he identified.

It defined how he would be recorded.

THE "ONE-DROP" FILES

By the early twentieth century, some state laws adopted strict definitions of racial classification. These statutes, preserved in legislative archives, specified how ancestry determined legal identity.

One of the most studied examples is the **Virginia Racial Integrity Act of 1924**, whose text survives in state legislative records. The act required that birth certificates and marriage licenses record racial identity according to statutory definitions.

Local registrars were instructed to enforce these classifications when issuing official documents.

In other words:

Identity became paperwork.

THE REGISTRARS

County clerks and registrars played a central role in this system. Their offices produced the documents that validated a person's legal existence:

Birth certificates.

Marriage licenses.

Death certificates.

Surviving correspondence between registrars and state agencies, preserved in state archive collections, shows that officials sometimes investigated ancestry claims before issuing documents.

These letters read like bureaucratic inquiries.

Requests for verification.

Requests for affidavits.

Requests for proof.

The tone is procedural.

The implications were life-altering.

WHEN RECORDS OVERRULED PEOPLE

Legal historians often emphasize a striking principle visible in archival cases: once an identity classification was recorded in official documents, it could outweigh personal testimony.

Court cases preserved in state judicial archives show individuals attempting to challenge how they were classified in official records. Some petitioned courts to amend birth registrations or marriage licenses.

The outcomes varied.

But the records show the same underlying reality:

The state considered documentation authoritative.

Not self-description.

THE CENSUS AS A MIRROR OF POWER

Census categories changed repeatedly across decades. Historians studying census schedules compare forms from different years and note how classification labels were added, removed, or redefined.

Each change reflected policy decisions.

Because census categories are not discovered.

They are chosen.

The U.S. Census Bureau preserves historical questionnaires and enumerator instructions that show precisely how census takers were directed to classify individuals during each decade.

The instructions were detailed.

And they were official.

THE POWER OF A CHECKBOX

Modern readers may overlook how much authority a simple checkbox can hold. Yet administrative historians point out that standardized forms are among the most influential tools governments possess.

Forms determine:

eligibility
status
recognition
rights
A box checked on a form can open doors.
Another can close them.
And once submitted, forms enter archives.

WHAT HISTORIANS SEE IN THE FILES

When scholars analyze historical classification records across multiple systems, census rolls, court documents, birth registries, legislative statutes, they often see something revealing:

Identity was not always treated as a personal characteristic.

It was treated as an administrative category.

That distinction matters because administrative categories can be changed without changing the people they describe.

And when categories change, so can rights.

THE ARCHIVE AS A RECORD OF DEFINITION

Few historical sources demonstrate institutional power more clearly than classification documents. They show how authorities defined populations at specific moments in time.

They do not argue.

They define.

They do not persuade.

They record.

And what they record tells historians not only how people lived, but how they were officially understood.

A name is personal.

An identity can be lived.

But once written into a government file, it becomes something else:

A legal fact.

END OF CHAPTER ANALYSIS

Education, Access, and the Record of Opportunity

The documents examined in this chapter reveal how access to education has historically been structured through administrative decision-making. Admission registers, school board minutes, funding allocations, examination requirements, and policy directives demonstrate that opportunity is rarely abstract. It is regulated.

Institutions do not merely open doors; they establish criteria for entry. Those criteria are written into bylaws, recorded in meeting minutes, and preserved in official publications. Once formalized, they become part of an enforceable framework. Eligibility, enrollment, and exclusion are not accidents when they appear repeatedly in documented procedure. They are systems.

From a legal perspective, educational records carry particular significance because courts have long recognized education as foundational to civic participation. When administrative policies affect access, those policies become subject to judicial review and legislative scrutiny. This is why educational documentation often appears in litigation and reform debates.

The archive shows that educational structures are built not only through curriculum but through classification. Funding categories, district boundaries, testing requirements, and admissions standards all generate paperwork. That paperwork reveals how opportunity was distributed, limited, or expanded.

Education is often described as the path forward. The record shows how that path was mapped.

LEGAL REFLECTION

Access is rarely accidental.

It is organized.

It is recorded.

And once recorded, it can be traced.

FINAL TRANSITION

The board minutes, admission records, and policy documents referenced in this chapter remain preserved in school archives, state repositories, and legislative collections. They exist as administrative artifacts, evidence of how educational opportunity was defined at particular moments in time.

They can still be reviewed.

The lesson was taught.

The ledger of access remained.

PRIMARY SOURCE DOSSIER VERIFIED ARCHIVES

Readers can independently consult:

• U.S. Census schedules and enumerator instructions — National Archives

• Virginia Racial Integrity Act (1924) — Virginia legislative archives

• Historical birth and marriage registries — state archives

• *Plessy v. Ferguson* (1896) — U.S. Supreme Court Reports

• State registrar correspondence collections — archival manuscript repositories

Chapter Fifteen

Chapter 15 THE FILES THAT DETERMINED MOVEMENT

When Permission Became a Requirement to Exist in Motion

Freedom is often imagined as a door opening.

But in many times and places, it has functioned more like a gate, one that opens only when someone else unlocks it.

Because movement is not merely physical.

It is administrative.

Travel requires permission.

Permission requires documentation.

Documentation requires approval.

And approval, once recorded, can be granted, or denied.

THE FIRST PASSES

Long before modern passports existed, authorities issued travel passes. During slavery, enslaved individuals were often required to carry written permission to move beyond designated areas. Surviving examples of these passes exist today in museum collections and manuscript archives.

After emancipation, the formal pass system did not remain identical, but historians note that various legal and administrative mechanisms continued to regulate movement in different ways.

Not always visibly.

Often bureaucratically.

THE VAGRANCY FILES RETURN

Post-Civil War vagrancy laws, preserved in state legislative archives, did more than define unemployment as an offense. In practice, they could restrict mobility.

Arrest logs and court records from the late nineteenth century show individuals detained for failing to demonstrate proof of residence or employment. These entries appear in county dockets as routine charges.

Historians studying these documents emphasize that such statutes functioned partly as tools of geographic control.

Because if a person can be arrested for not proving where they belong, movement becomes risky.

And risk restricts travel.

THE PASSPORT ERA

By the twentieth century, travel increasingly depended on standardized identification. Passport application files preserved in the U .S. National Archives contain forms listing:

name

birthplace

physical description

photograph

citizenship status

These applications were administrative necessities, but they also demonstrate how movement became linked to documentation.

You could not cross certain borders without a file.

And once a file existed, it could be reviewed.

THE INTERNAL MAPS

Mobility is not limited to international travel. Domestic movement has also been shaped by policy. During the early twentieth century, migration patterns within the United States were tracked through census data, railroad employment records, and labor department reports.

Historians analyzing these datasets often reconstruct migration flows by comparing population schedules across decades. These records show large-scale movements of people from rural to urban areas, from South to North, from agricultural work to industrial labor.

The data does not speculate.

It counts.

THE PERMITS THAT CONTROLLED ENTRY

Municipal archives from various cities preserve permit systems that regulated who could work, reside, or conduct business in particular districts. These permits appear in city council minutes, licensing ledgers, and municipal correspondence.

Such documents list:

applicant name

address

occupation

approval status

They read like administrative paperwork.

Because they were.

Yet historians studying urban governance often emphasize that licensing systems can function as gatekeepers. Approval determines access. Denial determines exclusion.

The permit is a piece of paper.

But it can shape a life.

THE COURTS AND THE RIGHT TO MOVE

Questions about mobility eventually reached federal courts. Among the most cited Supreme Court decisions on travel rights is:

Edwards v. California (1941)

The case record, preserved in United States Reports, addressed a California statute that criminalized bringing an indigent person into the state. The Court struck down the law, ruling that it violated constitutional principles.

The decision is important not only for its outcome but for what it demonstrates:

Mobility can become a legal question.

And when it does, it produces documents.

THE FILE AS A PASSPORT

Historians often note that in modern bureaucratic societies, movement rarely depends solely on physical ability. It depends on records.

Identification cards.

Licenses.

Certificates.

Permits.

Each document functions as proof.

Proof of identity.

Proof of status.

Proof of authorization.

Without proof, movement can stall.

With proof, it can proceed.

WHAT ARCHIVES SHOW ABOUT MOTION

When researchers compare travel regulations, licensing records, census migration data, and court rulings across decades, they observe a recurring pattern:

Movement is governed.

Not always by fences.

Often by forms.

The regulation of mobility rarely appears dramatic in official documents. It appears procedural. The language is technical. The tone is neutral.

Yet those procedures determine something fundamental:

Who can go.

And who cannot.

A locked door is obvious.

A denied document is quieter.

But both can stop a person in the same place.

END OF CHAPTER ANALYSIS

Movement, Permission, and the Documentation of Freedom

The materials examined in this chapter reveal how mobility has historically been shaped by administrative permission. Travel passes, residency registrations, migration records, internal permits, and passport applications demonstrate that movement is often governed not only by geography, but by documentation.

Freedom of movement is frequently assumed to be natural. The archive shows that it has often been procedural.

Institutions regulate mobility by establishing requirements: identification, approval, proof of status, proof of employment, proof of residence. Each requirement generates paperwork. That paperwork becomes the basis for determining who may move, when, and under what conditions.

From a legal standpoint, movement intersects with jurisdiction. Authorities require documentation to determine whether a person falls within their regulatory scope. Without papers, enforcement becomes uncertain. With papers, authority becomes precise.

The chapter's records illustrate that permission systems are rarely informal. They are structured through written procedures. Applications are reviewed. Decisions are recorded. Denials are documented. Approvals are filed. The administrative trail transforms movement into a governed act.

When permission becomes paperwork, mobility becomes measurable.

LEGAL REFLECTION

Freedom may be declared.

Permission is documented.

Where movement requires paper, authority follows the file.

FINAL TRANSITION

The permits, registries, and migration records referenced in this chapter remain preserved in national archives, immigration collections, and administrative repositories. They stand as documentary evidence of how movement was processed through institutional channels.

They remain accessible to researchers.

CINEMATIC CLOSING LINE

The road was open.

The paperwork decided who could take it.

PRIMARY SOURCE DOSSIER VERIFIED ARCHIVES

Readers can independently consult:

Historical travel passes — manuscript collections and museum archives

Post-Civil War vagrancy statutes — state legislative records

Passport application files — U.S. National Archives

Municipal licensing registers — city archives

Edwards v. California (1941) — U.S. Supreme Court Reports

Historical migration data — U.S. Census Bureau archives

Chapter Sixteen

Chapter 16 THE FILES THAT DETERMINED VOICE

When the Right to Speak Was Decided Before a Ballot Was Cast

A vote is silent.

No sound leaves the paper.

No echo follows the mark.

Yet few acts in civic life carry more power.

Because a vote does not only express a choice.

It records existence.

To be counted in a system is to be acknowledged by it. And for much of modern history, whether a person could be counted depended not on whether they were alive,

but whether they were allowed to be recorded.....

THE POLL BOOKS

In local archives across the United States sit long, narrow volumes known as **poll books**. They are not dramatic documents. Their pages contain simple lists:

Name.

Date.

District.

Status.

These books were administrative tools used by election officials to track who voted. Today they are preserved in state archives, county repositories, and historical societies.

Historians who study them often describe a moment of realization when they turn page after page and notice something striking:

Names appear.

Then they stop appearing.

Not gradually.

Abruptly.

WHEN LAW DEFININES THE BALLOT

After the Civil War, the Fifteenth Amendment to the United States Constitution declared that voting rights could not be denied on the basis of race. The amendment's text is preserved in federal archives and constitutional records.

On paper, the right existed.

But voting is not exercised on paper.

It is exercised in procedure.

State legislatures across the late nineteenth and early twentieth centuries enacted voting regulations that survive today in official statute books and legislative journals. These laws included requirements such as:

- literacy tests
- poll taxes
- residency documentation
- registration deadlines

Each requirement appeared administrative.

Each produced paperwork.

THE LITERACY TEST FORMS

Original literacy test sheets used in several states are preserved in museum collections and archival repositories. These forms required applicants to interpret passages of legal text or answer questions about constitutional provisions.

The tests were not standardized nationally. Surviving copies show that questions could vary widely depending on who administered them.

Historians examining these documents emphasize that their significance lies not in theory but in existence.

The forms are still there.

Typed. Printed. Filed.

THE TAX RECEIPTS

Poll tax systems required payment receipts before a ballot could be cast. Surviving tax registers and payment stubs exist in state archives and county record collections. These documents list:

payer name

amount

date

district

Without the receipt, a voter could be turned away.

The receipt was not symbolic.

It was proof.

And proof, once required, becomes a gate.

THE REGISTRATION LEDGERS

Election registration books preserved in local archives provide historians with some of the most detailed evidence of voting access. These ledgers recorded:

applicant names

approval status

rejection notes

Some entries include brief explanations written by registrars. Others list only a mark indicating acceptance or denial.

The handwriting is often neat. Methodical. Careful.

The clerk was doing their job.

Yet decades later, those entries allow researchers to reconstruct patterns across entire communities.

THE COURTROOM RETURNS ONCE MORE

Challenges to voting restrictions eventually reached federal courts. One of the most consequential legislative responses to documented barriers was the **Voting Rights Act of 1965**, whose full text is preserved in congressional archives and the United States Statutes at Large.

The law authorized federal oversight of voting procedures in certain jurisdictions and required documentation of election practices.

Once again, enforcement produced records.

Federal examiners filed reports.

Observers submitted notes.

Officials kept logs.

Each document became part of a growing archive showing how voting systems functioned in practice.

WHEN DATA REVEALS PARTICIPATION

Political historians often analyze historical voter participation using datasets compiled from election returns, census reports, and state voting statistics. When compared across decades, these records allow researchers to track changes in registration and turnout.

The power of these datasets lies in scale.

One number shows a result.

Thousands of numbers show a pattern.

And patterns are difficult to ignore.

THE POWER OF BEING COUNTED

Government systems depend on counts.

Population counts.

Tax counts.

Vote counts.

Being counted is not a small administrative detail. It determines representation, resource distribution, and political influence.

This is why historians often emphasize a simple but profound principle:

Counting is power.

Because what is counted is recognized.

And what is recognized can influence decisions.

WHAT THE ARCHIVES SHOW ABOUT VOICE

When scholars compare poll books, registration ledgers, literacy test forms, tax receipts, and court rulings across time, they see a layered record of how participation was structured.

No single document explains everything.

But together they reveal something unmistakable:

Voice, in civic systems, is never purely abstract.

It is administered.

And administration leaves files.

Speech can be silenced in a moment.

But a name entered, or missing, from a voting ledger can shape history for generations.

END OF CHAPTER ANALYSIS

Ballots, Barriers, and the Administration of Voice

The records examined in this chapter reveal that participation in civic life has long been governed through administrative mechanisms. Voting rolls, registration forms, literacy examinations, poll tax receipts, and procedural directives demonstrate that civic voice is not merely expressed, it is processed.

Institutions regulate participation through criteria. Eligibility requirements are codified. Verification procedures are established. Documentation is required. Each step generates a paper trail. That trail determines who is included in the official count and who is not.

From a legal perspective, voting documentation carries exceptional weight because it intersects directly with constitutional guarantees. When participation is conditioned on procedure, the procedure itself becomes a site of scrutiny. Courts review eligibility rules. Legislatures debate standards. Administrators record compliance.

The archive shows that civic participation is rarely informal. It is organized through paperwork. The ballot may be secret, but the eligibility process is not. Lists are compiled. Applications are approved or rejected. Receipts are issued. Records are preserved.

When voice becomes conditional on documentation, access to civic power flows through administrative channels.

LEGAL REFLECTION

The ballot speaks.

The registry decides who may cast it.

Where participation is recorded, authority shapes the count.

FINAL TRANSITION

The registration ledgers, testing forms, and election records referenced in this chapter remain preserved in state archives, county offices, and legislative repositories. They exist as tangible evidence of how civic access was structured and administered.

They can still be examined.

The vote was cast.

The record determined whether it counted.......

PRIMARY SOURCE DOSSIER VERIFIED ARCHIVES

Readers may consult:

- Historical poll books — state and county archives
- Literacy test forms — museum and university collections
- Poll tax registers — state archival records
- Voter registration ledgers — local election archives
- Voting Rights Act (1965) — U.S. Statutes at Large
- Federal election observer reports — National Archives

Chapter Seventeen

Chapter 17 THE FILES THAT DETERMINED SAFETY

When Protection Existed on Paper but Not in Practice

Safety is supposed to be the simplest promise a society makes.

Not prosperity.

Not power.

Just protection.

The assurance that if harm comes, someone will respond.

That if danger appears, someone will intervene.

That if a crime occurs, someone will act.

It is the most basic covenant between a government and its people.

And like every covenant in a bureaucratic state, it leaves paperwork.

THE REPORT THAT PROVES SOMETHING HAPPENED

Police reports are among the most routine documents ever produced. They are written daily, often quickly, usually without flourish. They list:

date

time

location

incident

action taken

Thousands of such reports from the nineteenth and twentieth centuries are preserved today in municipal archives, state repositories, and federal record groups.

Most are unremarkable.

Some are not.

Because occasionally, a report confirms that an event occurred, while simultaneously showing that nothing followed it.

THE RECORD OF RESPONSE

Historians studying law enforcement archives often examine two entries in particular:

Incident reported

Disposition

The first confirms that something happened.

The second reveals what was done.

In some preserved records, the disposition line reads:

no action

investigation suspended

insufficient grounds

These phrases are procedural. Standard. Administrative.

They do not describe emotion.

They describe outcome.

THE LOGBOOKS

Police station logbooks, some more than a century old, are among the most revealing historical documents because they were never meant for public reading. They were internal records used to track daily activity.

Surviving volumes show handwritten entries listing calls received, complaints filed, and officer assignments.

Historians who examine these books often notice a pattern:

Some incidents receive multiple follow-up entries.

Others receive only one.

The difference is not explained in the book.

It is simply recorded.

THE FEDERAL INVESTIGATIONS

At several points in American history, federal authorities reviewed local law enforcement conduct. The resulting reports, preserved in congressional archives and Department of Justice files, contain summaries of investigations into whether officials fulfilled their legal obligations.

These reports often include:

sworn testimony

correspondence

investigative notes

procedural findings

They are formal documents created through official inquiry. Their purpose was not storytelling. It was assessment.

Because when institutions investigate institutions, they produce records.

WHEN PROTECTION BECOMES JURISDICTION

Legal historians frequently point out that one of the most decisive factors in whether protection occurs is jurisdiction, the question of which authority is responsible for acting.

Court cases preserved in judicial archives show how often legal disputes hinged on this issue. Attorneys argued not only about what happened, but about who had the authority to respond.

Sometimes the result of a case turned not on facts, but on responsibility.

If no authority was determined to have jurisdiction, action could stall.

And when action stalls, records remain, but resolution does not.

THE DIFFERENCE BETWEEN POLICY AND PRACTICE

Official policies often state that all citizens are entitled to protection under the law. These policies appear in statutes, charters, and departmental manuals preserved in public archives.

But historians distinguish between policy and practice by comparing written rules with actual case outcomes.

This comparison requires documentation:

rules in one file

actions in another

Only when both are examined together does a pattern emerge.

THE COMMISSIONS THAT REVIEWED THE RECORD

Throughout the twentieth century, investigative commissions were occasionally formed to study episodes of violence or unrest. Their final reports—many publicly released and preserved in libraries and archives, compiled evidence from multiple sources.

These reports typically include:

timelines

witness testimony

official correspondence

statistical summaries

Because commissions gather information systematically, their findings often become some of the most comprehensive documentary records available for historians.

They do not rely on memory.

They rely on files.

WHAT RESEARCHERS SEE WHEN THEY COMPARE CASES

Modern scholars analyzing historical protection records often use comparative methods. They examine multiple incidents across different regions and time periods, drawing from:

police reports

court filings

investigative commissions

newspaper archives

municipal records

Individually, each document shows a single event.

Together, they show patterns of response.

And patterns of response reveal something crucial:

Not just what happened,

but what followed.

THE SILENCE THAT GETS WRITTEN DOWN

Absence is rarely visible in daily life.

But in archives, absence is measurable.

A missing arrest record.

An unsigned warrant.

A complaint without follow-up.

Archivists sometimes say that the most revealing documents are the ones that stop mid-process. They show where a procedure began but did not continue.

The file does not speculate why.

It simply ends.

WHY THESE FILES MATTER

The importance of protection records is not only what they document. It is what they demonstrate about systems:

Protection is not automatic.

It is administered.

And administration requires action.

When action occurs, it is recorded.

When it does not, that too can be recorded.

That is why historians study files.

Because files show not only events
but responses.

Danger can appear suddenly.

Protection is supposed to follow.

But history is written in the space between the two.

END OF CHAPTER ANALYSIS

Property, Ownership, and the Legal Definition of Belonging

The records examined in this chapter demonstrate how ownership is constructed through documentation. Deeds, titles, plats, tax rolls, foreclosure filings, and zoning maps reveal that property is not merely land or structure it is legal recognition recorded in official form.

Ownership depends on documentation. A claim to property becomes enforceable when it is entered into the registry. Without recordation, possession may be disputed. With recordation, it becomes recognized by the state.

From a legal perspective, property records are foundational. Courts rely on deeds and title chains to determine rightful ownership. Municipalities use tax rolls to allocate responsibility. Regulatory bodies consult zoning maps to define permitted use. Each document contributes to a system in which belonging is defined by paper.

The archive shows that property systems are structured through classification and recording. Boundaries are drawn. Names are entered. Transfers are notarized. Liens are filed. These processes convert physical space into regulated territory.

When property becomes documentation, access to land becomes dependent on administrative recognition.

LEGAL REFLECTION

Land exists in geography.

Ownership exists in record.

Where the deed is filed, authority is recognized.

FINAL TRANSITION

The deeds, tax records, and municipal filings referenced in this chapter remain preserved in county courthouses, land registries, and national archives. They stand as official evidence of how property rights were defined and administered at specific moments in time.

They remain available for review.

The ground did not move.

The paperwork determined who stood upon it.....

PRIMARY SOURCE DOSSIER VERIFIED ARCHIVES

Readers may consult:

Municipal police logbooks — city archives

Department of Justice investigative reports — National Archives

Congressional investigative commission reports — Library of Congress

State court jurisdiction rulings — judicial archives

Municipal charters and policing statutes — state repositories

Chapter Eighteen

Chapter 18
THE FILES THAT RECORDED DEATH

When the Final Record Became the Only Witness

Every system keeps a last document.

Not the first record.

Not the contract.

Not the charge.

The last one.

The record made when everything else has already happened.

Death certificates.

Coroner reports.

Burial registers.

These are the quietest documents in any archive.

They do not argue.

They do not accuse.

They conclude.

THE FINAL ENTRY

Death records are among the most standardized documents ever created. Across centuries, civil authorities required them for legal, medical, and statistical purposes. Surviving examples preserved in state archives and health department collections typically contain the same fields:

Name.

Date.

Location.

Cause.

Each entry is brief.

But historians often say the most revealing question is not what appears on the line,

It is how that line was filled in.

THE CORONER'S REPORT

Coroner inquest files, many dating back to the nineteenth century, are preserved in county archives throughout the United States. These reports were created when deaths occurred under unusual or suspicious circumstances.

They often include:

witness statements

physician observations

jury conclusions

official determinations

The tone is procedural. Clinical. Formal.

Because the coroner's task was not to speculate.

It was to record findings.

And findings, once written, become official history.

THE LANGUAGE OF CAUSE

Medical historians frequently analyze the wording used in historical death records. Over time, official terminology has changed, reflecting evolving standards of medicine and law.

Earlier records sometimes used broad categories such as:

natural causes

accident

unknown

exposure

violence

Later records became more specific as forensic science advanced.

Researchers compare these categories across decades to study how causes of death were documented and classified. The changes reveal not only medical progress, but shifts in investigative practice.

Because classification shapes interpretation.

THE REGISTERS OF THE UNCLAIMED

In municipal archives and cemetery records, historians sometimes encounter burial ledgers listing individuals buried without family claims. These entries are often minimal:

Date.

Location.

Identifier.

Some contain no name at all.

Such records were administrative necessities. Cities were required to document burials for public health and legal purposes. Yet for historians, they provide insight into how societies handled death at the margins.

Even anonymity leaves a record.

THE INVESTIGATIVE COMMISSIONS

At several points in American history, large-scale investigations examined violent incidents that resulted in multiple deaths. Official commissions produced detailed reports summarizing evidence gathered from police files, medical records, witness testimony, and photographic documentation.

These reports, preserved in libraries, archives, and government repositories, often include:

timelines

casualty lists

medical findings

official conclusions

They are among the most comprehensive historical sources because they compile information from many independent records into a single documented account.

They do not rely on memory.

They rely on files.

WHEN STATISTICS BECOME HISTORY

Public health agencies have long compiled mortality statistics. Annual mortality tables published by state and federal offices, many digitized today, list causes of death across populations and time periods.

Historians analyzing these datasets often track long-term trends:

life expectancy

disease rates

injury deaths

Each table represents thousands of individual records combined into a statistical snapshot.

One certificate shows a life ended.

Thousands of certificates show a pattern.

THE POWER OF DOCUMENTED FINALITY

Unlike most historical records, death records carry a unique authority. They mark an event that cannot be reversed or revised.

A contract can be amended.

A charge can be dismissed.

A verdict can be appealed.

But a death entry is final.

That finality gives these documents a particular weight for historians. They represent the end point of systems, decisions, and circumstances that may have begun long before the final entry was written.

WHAT RESEARCHERS SEE IN THE FILES

When scholars compare coroner reports, burial logs, death certificates, investigative findings, and statistical tables, they often observe how multiple layers of documentation interact.

A coroner's conclusion may appear in one file.

A police report in another.

A public health table in a third.

Together, they form a composite record.

No single document explains everything.

But the archive, taken as a whole, speaks.

THE CLERK WHO WROTE THE LAST LINE

As in so many historical systems, the final entry was usually written not by a judge or a politician, but by a clerk.

A clerk who recorded the name.

A clerk who noted the date.

A clerk who closed the file.

The clerk did not write history intentionally.

Yet without that entry, history would lose its ending.

A life can end in an instant.

But once its last line is entered into the record, it becomes permanent.

And permanence is the archive's strongest voice.

END OF CHAPTER ANALYSIS

Confinement, Custody, and the Documentation of Control

The materials examined in this chapter reveal how confinement becomes formalized through documentation. Intake records, sentencing forms, disciplinary reports, transfer orders, and release certificates demonstrate that custody is not simply physical restriction it is an administrative status recorded in official files.

Institutions that exercise custodial authority rely heavily on paperwork. A sentence must be entered. A commitment order must be signed. A transfer must be logged. Each step creates a traceable record that allows the institution to justify continued control.

From a legal standpoint, confinement exists at the intersection of statutory authority and procedural compliance. Courts issue judgments. Correctional institutions implement them. Administrative records preserve the timeline. If a record is incomplete, authority may be questioned. If it is intact, authority appears validated.

The archive shows that confinement systems are structured through meticulous documentation. Reports accumulate. Evaluations are filed. Incidents are logged. Reviews are conducted. This accumulation of paperwork forms a narrative of custody a narrative written by the institution itself.

When the status of confinement is recorded, it becomes enforceable across time and personnel. The file does not leave when the officer leaves. The status does not vanish when the shift changes.

Documentation sustains custody.

LEGAL REFLECTION

The door may close once.

The file keeps it closed.

Where confinement is recorded, authority is preserved.

FINAL TRANSITION

The commitment orders, institutional logs, and administrative records discussed in this chapter remain preserved in court archives, correctional repositories, and government record groups. They stand as documentary evidence of how custody was processed and maintained.

They remain open to examination.

The cell contained the body.

The paperwork contained the authority.....

PRIMARY SOURCE DOSSIER VERIFIED ARCHIVAL RECORDS

Readers may consult:

State death certificate registries — public health archives

County coroner inquest files — local historical repositories

Municipal burial ledgers — city archive collections

Government investigative commission reports — library and federal archives

Historical mortality tables — public health statistical publications

Chapter Nineteen

Chapter 19 THE FILES THAT MEASURED A PEOPLE

When Entire Lives Became Data

One record can describe a person.

A thousand records can describe a community.

Millions can describe a nation.

Because when governments, institutions, and researchers stop documenting individuals and begin documenting populations, something changes. The file is no longer about a life.

It becomes about a pattern.

And patterns are powerful.

They can shape policy.

They can influence law.

They can justify decisions.

All without ever naming a single person.

THE FIRST NATIONAL COUNTS

Long before modern data science existed, governments collected population statistics. Census schedules preserved in the National Archives show that early enumerations did not simply count inhabitants. They categorized them.

Age.

Sex.

Occupation.

Status.

Historians emphasize that census-taking has always been more than counting. It is classification combined with measurement. The numbers produced by a census determine representation, taxation, and funding.

In other words:

Counting people helps determine how power is distributed among them.

WHEN NUMBERS BECOME POLICY

Statistical tables compiled from census returns often informed legislation. Lawmakers relied on demographic reports to understand population distribution, economic conditions, and labor supply.

These reports, preserved in congressional records and federal statistical publications, contain page after page of numbers arranged in columns. At first glance, they look dry and technical.

But historians note something crucial:

Numbers can influence decisions without appearing to argue.

A statistic does not demand action.

It suggests it.

And suggestion can shape policy just as effectively as persuasion.

THE BIRTH OF SOCIAL STATISTICS

By the late nineteenth century, government agencies began producing annual statistical abstracts summarizing national data. These publications, many digitized today through federal archives, compiled information on:

employment

wages

mortality

education

migration

Each edition compared current figures with previous years.

This comparison turned raw numbers into trends.

And trends tell stories.

THE POWER OF A TREND LINE

A single year's data shows a moment.

Ten years show a direction.

Fifty years show a trajectory.

Researchers who study long-term datasets often rely on historical statistical reports because they provide continuity across generations. When numbers are recorded consistently over decades, they allow historians to track change with unusual precision.

They can see:

growth

decline

stability

disparity

Not from opinion

From measurement.

THE FILE WITHOUT NAMES

One of the most striking features of population statistics is their anonymity. Most demographic tables contain no individual names. Instead, they aggregate thousands or millions of entries into totals.

This anonymity has a paradoxical effect.

It removes personal identity.

But it reveals collective reality.

A single record can be dismissed as anecdotal.

A dataset containing millions cannot.

THE MAPS OF DATA

As statistical methods advanced in the twentieth century, agencies began presenting demographic information visually. Charts, graphs, and maps, preserved in government reports and academic publications, translated numerical tables into images.

Historians studying these materials often note how visual data can reveal relationships that raw numbers alone do not show.

A map can display concentration.

A graph can display change.

A chart can display comparison.

Visualization does not create information.

It clarifies it.

THE ROLE OF FEDERAL DATA COLLECTION

Modern demographic research often relies on datasets compiled by agencies such as the U.S. Census Bureau and the National Center for Health Statistics. These agencies preserve decades of historical data accessible through public archives.

Scholars use these datasets to analyze long-term patterns in:

population growth

income distribution

education levels

health outcomes

The conclusions drawn from such research are not speculative.

They are calculated.

WHAT HISTORIANS SEE WHEN THEY STACK DATA

One dataset shows one dimension.

Multiple datasets stacked together reveal relationships.

For example, historians may compare:

census data

school enrollment reports

employment statistics

mortality tables

Individually, each dataset describes one aspect of life.

Combined, they show structure.

That structure can reveal how systems affect populations across time.

THE AUTHORITY OF ACCUMULATION

Numbers gain authority not because they are numbers, but because they accumulate. The longer a system records data, the more powerful that data becomes as historical evidence.

A single figure can be questioned.

A century of figures becomes a record.

And records carry weight.

Because they can be checked.

THE ARCHIVE AS A POPULATION MEMORY

Personal memory fades. Oral history can disappear. Individual testimony may be lost.

But statistical archives preserve something different:

Collective memory.

They store information about entire populations long after the individuals within those populations are gone. They record births, deaths, migrations, occupations, and conditions across generations.

In doing so, they create a form of historical memory that does not rely on storytelling.

It relies on counting.

A person can be forgotten.

A number can be ignored.

But millions of numbers, recorded year after year, become something else entirely:

Evidence.

END OF CHAPTER ANALYSIS

Health, Public Policy, and the Institutional Management of Risk

The documents examined in this chapter reveal how public health systems convert vulnerability into administrative categories. Hospital intake records, health board directives, quarantine notices, insurance determinations, and epidemiological reports demonstrate that illness is not treated solely as a private condition. It becomes a matter of public regulation.

Public health authority operates through documentation. Diagnoses are recorded. Exposure lists are compiled. Treatment protocols are issued. Risk assessments are calculated. These written instruments allow institutions to justify intervention whether through treatment, isolation, allocation of resources, or denial of services.

From a legal perspective, public health authority rests on statutory delegation. Legislatures empower agencies to act in the name of collective safety. Agencies document their actions to demonstrate compliance with that delegation. Courts reviewing such actions rely heavily on the written record. If the record shows procedural adherence, institutional decisions are often upheld.

The archive reveals that public health administration is built upon risk classification. Groups are identified. Conditions are categorized. Outcomes are tracked. These processes create a framework in which medical and legal authority intersect.

When risk becomes documented, it becomes governable.

LEGAL REFLECTION

Illness may begin in the body.

Authority begins in the file.

Where risk is recorded, regulation follows.

FINAL TRANSITION

The health board minutes, hospital registries, and public policy directives referenced in this chapter remain preserved in medical archives, municipal repositories, and national record collections. They exist as contemporaneous documentation of how institutions responded to vulnerability through administrative structure.

They remain accessible to researchers.

The diagnosis was written.

The policy was enacted.....

PRIMARY SOURCE DOSSIER VERIFIED ARCHIVAL SOURCES

Readers may consult:

U.S. Census historical schedules — National Archives

Statistical Abstracts of the United States — federal publications

Congressional demographic reports — Library of Congress

National Center for Health Statistics datasets — federal archives

Historical labor and education statistics — Department of Commerce publications

Chapter Twenty

Chapter 20
THE FILES THAT EXPLAINED THE NUMBERS

When Data Began Speaking in the Language of Authority

Numbers by themselves are quiet.

They sit in tables.

They rest in columns.

They wait in rows.

They do not announce what they mean.

Someone has to interpret them.

And the moment interpretation begins, a new kind of document appears—one that does not merely record reality, but explains it.

Reports.

Studies.

Analyses.

Findings.

These are the files that tell society what its numbers are supposed to say.

THE RISE OF THE REPORT

By the late nineteenth and early twentieth centuries, government agencies and research institutions increasingly produced analytical reports based on collected data. These publications, preserved in federal archives, university libraries, and legislative repositories, examined population statistics and offered conclusions.

They often contained sections titled:

Findings

Interpretation

Recommendations

This structure marked a shift.

Earlier documents counted people.

These documents evaluated them.

WHEN ANALYSIS BECOMES POLICY

Lawmakers frequently relied on analytical reports when drafting legislation. Congressional records show that committees requested studies from agencies, commissions, and research boards before proposing new laws.

These reports were not informal.

They were bound volumes submitted as official documents. Many survive today in the Government Publishing Office archives and Library of Congress collections.

Historians who examine legislative history often note that such reports served as bridges between raw data and public policy.

Because before a policy is enacted, someone must explain why it should exist.

THE LANGUAGE OF AUTHORITY

Analytical reports tend to share a recognizable tone. Unlike speeches or editorials, they are written in technical language designed to appear objective. Common phrases include:

according to data

statistical analysis indicates

the findings suggest

This language matters.

Not because it proves conclusions are correct.

But because it signals authority.

Readers encountering such phrasing often assume that the statements rest on measurement, calculation, and expertise. And when a document appears authoritative, it carries influence beyond its pages.

THE ACADEMIC ARCHIVES

Universities became major centers for data interpretation in the twentieth century. Academic journals, many preserved in digital scholarly databases and research libraries, published studies analyzing social, economic, and demographic data.

These articles typically include:

methodology

datasets

statistical models

conclusions

Scholars reviewing historical journals often note that academic studies can shape public understanding even when they do not directly change laws. Their influence spreads through citation.

One study references another.

That study references a third.

Over time, a network of interpretation forms.

THE POWER OF CITATION

Historians of knowledge often emphasize that citation functions as a form of institutional memory. When a report or study is cited repeatedly, it gains credibility. Not because it is repeated, but because it is referenced.

This process leaves a traceable record.

Footnotes.

Bibliographies.

References.

Each citation shows how ideas travel through time. Researchers can follow these references backward, tracing how conclusions evolved from earlier data.

In this way, interpretation itself becomes documented.

THE GOVERNMENT STUDY

Throughout the twentieth century, federal agencies commissioned large-scale studies examining national conditions. These studies, preserved in archival collections, analyzed issues such as employment, education, health, and housing.

They often combined multiple data sources:

census figures

administrative records

survey responses

Because they synthesized information from many datasets, these reports sometimes became foundational references for later researchers and policymakers.

The significance of such studies lies not only in their conclusions, but in their methodology, which is typically documented in detail.

WHEN INTERPRETATION SHAPES REALITY

Interpretation does not remain abstract. Once findings appear in official reports, they can influence decisions about funding, enforcement, and regulation.

Historians frequently observe that interpretation can be as powerful as measurement. The same dataset can produce different conclusions depending on how it is analyzed.

This is why archival reports are so valuable to researchers.

They reveal not only what was known,

but how it was understood.

THE FILE AS AN ARGUMENT

Unlike raw statistics, analytical reports often function as structured arguments. They present evidence, draw conclusions, and sometimes recommend action.

This transforms the document's role.

It is no longer a passive record.

It is an active instrument.

It can persuade legislators.

Guide agencies.

Inform courts.

The file becomes a participant in decision-making.

WHAT HISTORIANS SEE IN INTERPRETIVE RECORDS

When scholars compare analytical reports across decades, they often notice changes in interpretation even when underlying data remains similar.

This reveals something essential:

Data does not speak for itself.

People speak for it.

And when they do, they leave behind a written explanation of what they believed the numbers meant at that moment in history.

Those explanations become part of the archive.

THE ACCUMULATION OF EXPLANATION

Over time, interpretations accumulate just as raw data does. A single report becomes one voice among many. Dozens of reports form a conversation. Hundreds form a tradition of analysis.

Future researchers can examine this tradition to understand not only historical conditions, but historical thinking.

Because archives preserve ideas as carefully as they preserve events.

Numbers record what happened.

Reports explain what it meant.

And history is written where those two meet.

END OF CHAPTER ANALYSIS

Narrative, Memory, and the Power to Define History

The materials examined in this chapter reveal that institutions do not only regulate through law and procedure. They also regulate through narrative. Official reports, commission findings, press releases, public statements, and historical summaries demonstrate that the written explanation of events can shape collective understanding as profoundly as the events themselves.

Narrative becomes authoritative when it is documented by recognized institutions. Once entered into official publications, interpretations gain legitimacy. They may be cited in court opinions, legislative debates, educational materials, and media coverage. Over time, repetition transforms interpretation into accepted account.

From a legal standpoint, official narratives often function as background context in judicial reasoning. Courts rely on government reports. Legislatures reference commission findings. Policymakers consult historical summaries when drafting reforms. The archive shows that the act of documenting interpretation can influence future action.

Memory that is institutionalized acquires structure. It is indexed, published, and preserved. Alternative accounts may exist, but the officially recorded version carries procedural weight because it is attached to recognized authority.

This chapter demonstrates that documentation does not merely record events. It frames them.

LEGAL REFLECTION

Events occur once.

Narratives endure.

What is written into the record can shape how the event is remembered.

FINAL TRANSITION

The commission reports, public statements, and institutional summaries referenced in this chapter remain housed in government archives, university libraries, and digital repositories. They stand as preserved articulations of how events were officially interpreted at the time.

They can still be examined and compared.

The story was written.

History decided which version would be filed.....

PRIMARY SOURCE DOSSIER VERIFIED ARCHIVAL SOURCES

Readers may consult:

Congressional committee reports — Library of Congress

Federal agency analytical studies — National Archives

Government Publishing Office historical publications

Academic journal archives — university library collections
Statistical interpretation reports — federal research agencies

Epilogue

EPILOGUE

The Ink That Outlived Its Authors

Empires fall.

Governments collapse.

Institutions dissolve.

Names of powerful men fade into footnotes.

But documents remain.

The signatures placed upon official records long ago still exist in ink that has not yet surrendered to time. The individuals who wrote them may be gone, but their handwriting remains as testimony.

History does not only survive in monuments.

It survives in files.

What we inherit from the past is not merely memory. It is documentation. And documentation does something memory cannot, it refuses to change its story.

Long after voices have been silenced, records continue speaking.

They speak to anyone willing to read them.

The truth is rarely hidden. More often, it is archived.

The question is not whether evidence exists.

The question is whether anyone will open the drawer.

ARCHIVAL APPENDIX

ARCHIVAL APPENDIX

Primary Documentary Sources by Chapter

CHAPTER 1 — MARITIME CRIMES & THE ZONG

Primary Case

Gregson v. Gilbert (1783)

Archives

• UK National Archives — Record Series KB, C, HCA

• Lloyd's of London Archive — Marine Insurance Ledgers (1780–1785)

• National Maritime Museum Caird Library — West Indies trade vessels

• Douglas's Reports (1783 law reports)

Search Terms

Zong / Zorg / Cöllingwood / Liverpool slave ship / insurance loss claim

CHAPTER 2 — POST-SLAVERY FORCED LABOR SYSTEMS

Primary Records

• US National Archives — Record Group 60 (Department of Justice)

• Peonage Case Files (1901–1945)

• Federal District Court Indictments

Search Terms

Peonage / involuntary servitude / debt labor prosecutions

CHAPTER 3 — VAGRANCY & CONTROL STATUTES

Primary Sources

• State legislative session laws (1865–1910)

• County arrest dockets

• Freedmen's Bureau complaints

Archives

• National Archives RG 105 — Freedmen's Bureau

• State Archives (Southern states)

CHAPTER 4 — IDENTIFICATION & CONTROL DOCUMENTS

Records

• Early internal passport laws

• Labor pass systems

• Convict lease records

Archives

• State penitentiary archives

• Department of Corrections historical ledgers

CHAPTER 5 — REGULATION OF MOVEMENT

Sources

• Municipal residency permits

• Labor registration cards

• Interstate migration reports

Repositories

• City archives (Chicago, Atlanta, New Orleans, Birmingham)

• Library of Congress migration collections

CHAPTER 6 — POLICING RECORDS & PROTECTION FILES

Primary Evidence

• Police blotters

• Incident logs

• Officer reports

Archives

• Municipal police historical units

• City Clerk Record Offices

CHAPTER 7 — FEDERAL INVESTIGATIONS

Key Sources

• DOJ investigative memoranda

• Congressional inquiry reports

Archive

US National Archives

Record Groups:

• RG 60 — Justice Department

• RG 233 — House Committee Records

CHAPTER 8 — UNPROSECUTED VIOLENCE CASES

Records

• Grand jury proceedings

• Declination memoranda

• Closed investigation notices

Repositories

• County courthouse archives

• Federal District Court archives

CHAPTER 9 — MEDICAL CONTROL & EXPERIMENTATION

Primary Sources

• Public health department records

• Hospital administrative files

• Institutional review case records

Archives

• National Library of Medicine

• State hospital archives

Key Reference Work:

Harriet A. Washington — *Medical Apartheid*

CHAPTER 10 — MORTALITY RECORDS

Documents

• Death certificates

• Coroner inquest reports

• Burial registers

Archives

• County Vital Records Offices

• State Health Departments

• Historical cemetery registries

CHAPTER 11 — STATISTICAL CONTROL

Primary Data

• US Census historical schedules

• Labor statistics reports

• Mortality tables

Archives

• US Census Bureau Historical Division

• Bureau of Labor Statistics Historical Reports

CHAPTER 12 — BODY REGULATION FILES

Records

• Institutional confinement records

• Prison medical logs

• Workhouse registers

Repositories

- State archives
- Department of Corrections historical files

CHAPTER 13 — ECONOMIC CONTROL DOCUMENTS

Sources

- Wage contracts
- Sharecropping agreements
- Debt ledgers

Archives

- Plantation papers collections
- Agricultural extension archives
- University special collections

CHAPTER 14 — EDUCATIONAL ACCESS FILES

Records

- School board minutes
- Admission registers
- Literacy test forms

Repositories

- State education archives
- Local board of education records

CHAPTER 15 — MOVEMENT AUTHORIZATION FILES

Sources

- Travel permits
- Internal migration permits
- Passport applications

Archives

- National Archives passport files
- Immigration and Naturalization historical records

CHAPTER 16 — VOTING RECORDS

Primary Documents

- Poll books
- Voter registration ledgers
- Literacy test forms
- Poll tax receipts

Repositories

- State election archives
- County registrars' offices

Key Federal Law Source:

Voting Rights Act (1965) — US Statutes at Large

CHAPTER 17 — PROTECTION FAILURE FILES

Records

- Police disposition logs
- Complaint reports
- Investigative summaries

Archives

- Municipal police archives
- DOJ Civil Rights Division records

CHAPTER 18 — CORONER & DEATH INVESTIGATION FILES

Primary Evidence

- Inquest transcripts
- Medical examiner reports
- Autopsy registers

Repositories

- County coroner archives
- State forensic offices

CHAPTER 19 — POPULATION DATA FILES

Sources

- Statistical Abstract of the United States
- Census microdata

• Health statistics tables

Archives

• National Archives statistical publications

• Government Printing Office historical series

CHAPTER 20 — ANALYTICAL GOVERNMENT REPORTS

Primary Documents

• Congressional committee reports

• Federal research studies

• Policy analysis memoranda

Repositories

• Library of Congress Congressional Record collections

• Government Publishing Office archives

CHAPTER 21 — DECISION FILES

Core Records

• Judicial opinions

• Executive directives

• Prosecutorial decisions

Key Case Example

Federal review of Emmett Till investigation

Archives

• DOJ Civil Rights Division case files

• Federal court records

• State court archives

RESEARCH AUTHENTICATION STANDARD (INSERT SECTION)

Professional historians verify historical claims when at least **three independent primary sources**confirm an event:

Type

Example

Administrative

registry or ledger

Legal

court or indictment

Commercial

contract or insurance

External

newspaper or letter

RESEARCH METHOD STATEMENT

This work is grounded in primary documentation preserved in national, state, municipal, and institutional archives. Every major claim corresponds to surviving records created contemporaneously by governing, commercial, or legal authorities. Readers are encouraged to consult the archival collections listed to verify evidence independently.

ANNOTATED BIBLIOGRAPHY

Primary Sources, Archival Collections, and Foundational Scholarship

I. MARITIME LAW & THE ZONG CASE

Douglas, Sylvester. Reports of Cases Argued and Determined in the Court of King's Bench (1783). London.

This volume contains the published legal summary of *Gregson v. Gilbert*, commonly known as the Zong case. The report documents arguments made before the King's Bench and reveals that the dispute was treated as an insurance claim.

Why it matters: This is one of the earliest printed legal records of the case.

Verification: Available in major law libraries, British Library Rare Books collection, and university legal archives.

The National Archives (UK). King's Bench Records (KB series), High Court of Admiralty (HCA series), Chancery (C series).

These record groups preserve court filings, depositions, and maritime dispute documentation.

Why it matters: They contain the underlying legal paperwork behind printed reports.

Verification: Accessible via the National Archives catalogue at Kew. Researchers may request files by series and year.

Lloyd's of London Archive. Marine Insurance Underwriting Ledgers (late 18th century).

Insurance underwriting books and maritime loss claims.

Why it matters: The Zong case was fundamentally an insurance dispute; these ledgers confirm how losses were categorized.

Verification: Access by formal archival request to Lloyd's Archive.

Trans-Atlantic Slave Trade Database. Emory University and consortium partners.

A peer-reviewed digital database compiling voyage records from maritime archives worldwide.

Why it matters: Confirms ship names, voyage dates, captains, ports, and mortality rates.

Verification: Searchable by ship name (Zong / Zorg), captain (Luke Collingwood), year (1781).

II. POST-EMANCIPATION FORCED LABOR

United States National Archives. Record Group 60 (Department of Justice). Peonage Case Files, 1901–1945.

Contains indictments, investigative memoranda, and prosecution records involving involuntary servitude cases after slavery.

Why it matters: Demonstrates continuation of forced labor under new legal mechanisms.

Verification: Available through National Archives finding aids under RG 60.

United States National Archives. Record Group 105 (Freedmen's Bureau).

Includes labor contracts, complaints of abuse, and reports of coercion from formerly enslaved individuals.

Why it matters: Provides contemporaneous testimony about early post-slavery exploitation.

Verification: Digitized portions available; physical records housed in Washington, D.C.

III. CONVICT LEASING & VAGRANCY STATUTES

Blackmon, Douglas A. Slavery by Another Name. New York: Anchor Books, 2008.

Extensively documents forced labor prosecutions and peonage through archival research.

Why it matters: Connects archival DOJ files to broader systemic patterns.

Verification: Citations traceable to federal case files and newspaper archives.

State Legislative Session Laws (Southern States, 1865–1900).

Printed volumes of post-Civil War laws, including vagrancy statutes.

Why it matters: Shows how legal frameworks criminalized unemployment and mobility.

Verification: Held in state archives and law libraries.

IV. MEDICAL CONTROL & EXPERIMENTATION

Washington, Harriet A. Medical Apartheid. New York: Doubleday, 2007.

Documents centuries of medical exploitation of Black Americans using primary medical and institutional records.

Why it matters: Provides sourced evidence of systemic medical abuse.

Verification: Citations trace to National Library of Medicine, hospital archives, and government reports.

National Library of Medicine Archives.

Preserves public health studies, institutional research documentation, and hospital administrative records.

Why it matters: Primary repository for federal medical documentation.

Verification: On-site research and digital catalog access.

V. CIVIL RIGHTS INVESTIGATIONS & COLD CASES

United States Department of Justice. Civil Rights Division. Federal Review of the Emmett Till Case (2004; reopened 2017; closed 2021).

Official memoranda explaining investigative steps and reasons for closure.

Why it matters: Demonstrates how modern authorities evaluate historical crimes.

Verification: Public DOJ records; archived press releases and reports.

Mississippi State Archives. Court Records (1955 Emmett Till trial).

Trial transcripts, indictment records, and jury verdict documentation.

Why it matters: Provides original courtroom documentation.

Verification: Mississippi Department of Archives and History.

VI. POPULATION & STATISTICAL RECORDS

United States Census Bureau. Historical Census Schedules (1790–1950).

Population counts, demographic classifications, labor categories.

Why it matters: Shows how racial categories were officially defined and tabulated.

Verification: Available through National Archives microfilm collections.

Bureau of Labor Statistics. Historical Bulletins.

Labor participation and wage data.

Why it matters: Quantifies economic disparities documented narratively in the book.

Verification: Government Printing Office archives.

VII. CONGRESSIONAL & POLICY RECORDS

Congressional Record (1873–present).

Official transcript of debates and legislation.

Why it matters: Reveals legislative reasoning and intent.

Verification: Library of Congress collections.

United States Statutes at Large.

Official publication of federal laws.

Why it matters: Confirms statutory language governing labor, voting, and civil rights.

Verification: Public law volumes in federal repositories.

VIII. RESEARCH METHODOLOGY NOTE

This bibliography prioritizes:

1. Primary government records
2. Contemporary legal reports
3. Archival maritime documentation
4. Peer-reviewed scholarship built from original files

Where possible, claims are traceable to:

- Court transcripts
- Administrative records
- Insurance ledgers
- Legislative statutes

• Census data

AUTHOR'S EVIDENTIARY STANDARD

This work relies on documentation created by:

• Courts

• Legislatures

• Maritime insurers

• Government departments

• Institutional administrators

The sources cited are preserved in national archives, law libraries, and research institutions. Readers are encouraged to consult these collections directly.

FOOTNOTES EDITION

(Place as footnotes in your book)

Maritime / Zong Case

1. Sylvester Douglas, *Reports of Cases Argued and Determined in the Court of King's Bench* (London, 1783).

2. The National Archives (UK), King's Bench Records, KB series, case materials relating to *Gregson v. Gilbert* (1783).

3. The National Archives (UK), High Court of Admiralty Records, HCA series, late eighteenth-century maritime disputes.

4. Lloyd's of London Archive, Marine Insurance Ledgers, 1780–1785.

5. Trans-Atlantic Slave Trade Database, voyage entry for ship *Zong* (1781).

Forced Labor / Peonage

6. United States National Archives, Record Group 60, Department of Justice, Peonage Case Files, 1901–1945.

7. United States National Archives, Record Group 105, Freedmen's Bureau Records, labor complaints and contract disputes, 1865–1872.

8. Douglas A. Blackmon, *Slavery by Another Name* (New York: Anchor Books, 2008).

Legal & Legislative Systems

9. *United States Statutes at Large*, vols. covering Reconstruction-era legislation.

10. *Congressional Record*, various sessions, late nineteenth and twentieth centuries.

Medical Documentation

11. Harriet A. Washington, *Medical Apartheid* (New York: Doubleday, 2007).

12. National Library of Medicine Archives, historical institutional medical records collections.

Census & Statistical Data

13. United States Census Bureau, Historical Census Schedules, 1790–1950.

14. Bureau of Labor Statistics, Historical Bulletins, various years.

Civil Rights Investigations

15. United States Department of Justice, Civil Rights Division, federal review materials relating to the Emmett Till investigation (2004–2021).

16. Mississippi Department of Archives and History, trial records, *State of Mississippi v. Milam and Bryant* (1955).

PART II — BLUEBOOK LEGAL CITATION EDITION

(Use in legal-style notes, appendices, or law-review-style edition)

Cases

Gregson v. Gilbert, 3 Doug. 232 (K.B. 1783).

State v. Milam & Bryant, No. 1955-Trial Records (Miss. Cir. Ct. 1955).

Statutes

U.S. Const. amend. XV.

Voting Rights Act of 1965, Pub. L. No. 89-110, 79 Stat. 437.

Reconstruction Acts, 14 Stat. 428 (1867).

Government Records

U.S. Dep't of Justice, Peonage Files, Record Group 60, Nat'l Archives.

Freedmen's Bureau Records, Record Group 105, Nat'l Archives.

U.S. Dep't of Justice, Civil Rights Division, Emmett Till Investigation Files (2004–2021).

Historical Government Publications

U.S. Census Bureau, Historical Census Publications (1790–1950).

Bureau of Labor Statistics, Historical Reports Series.

Archival Sources

The National Archives (UK), King's Bench Records (KB Series).

The National Archives (UK), High Court of Admiralty Records (HCA Series).

Lloyd's of London Archive, Marine Insurance Ledgers (18th Century).

National Library of Medicine, Historical Medical Archives Collection.

CITATION STANDARD STATEMENT FOR BOOK

This work employs both Chicago historical citation style and Bluebook legal citation format. Chicago references document historical sources and archival materials. Bluebook citations document legal authorities, statutes, and court decisions. This dual-citation method allows verification through both academic and legal research standards.

PRIMARY SOURCE INDEX

Archive Series, Record Groups, Box Guidance & Retrieval Structure

(Expert-Witness / Investigative Grade)

This section is formatted for inclusion at the back of your book. It does not rely on hyperlinks. It provides institutional locations, record series names, and retrieval instructions.

PART I

UNITED KINGDOM ARCHIVES

A. The National Archives (Kew, Richmond, Surrey)

1. King's Bench Records (KB Series)

Relevant to: Zong litigation; maritime insurance dispute proceedings

Time Period: 1780–1785

Search Under:

• KB 122 (King's Bench pleadings)

• KB 127 (case records, late 18th century)

• Case name: *Gregson v. Gilbert*

Material Type:

• Pleadings

• Depositions

• Trial summaries

• Judicial rulings

2. High Court of Admiralty (HCA Series)

Relevant to: Maritime disputes, ship seizures, commercial shipping matters

Search Under:

• HCA 1 (Instance Court)

• HCA 13 (Appeal Court)

• Maritime insurance disputes (1780s)

3. Chancery Records (C Series)

Relevant to: Commercial equity disputes

Use When: Searching insurance or commercial contract litigation

B. Lloyd's of London Archive

Collection:

Marine Insurance Underwriting Books (1770–1790)

Search Terms:

- Zong
- Zorg
- Luke Collingwood
- West Indies voyage
- Marine loss claims

Material Type:

- Underwriting subscription entries
- Risk calculations
- Loss classifications
- Claim correspondence

Access requires formal research application.

C. National Maritime Museum (Greenwich)

Archive Section: Caird Library & Archive

Search Categories:

- West India merchant vessels
- Liverpool slave ships (1780–1783)
- Crew lists
- Vessel registration papers

PART II

UNITED STATES NATIONAL ARCHIVES

A. Record Group 60 — Department of Justice

Title: General Records of the Department of Justice

Key Series:

- Peonage Case Files (1901–1945)
- Civil Rights Investigative Memoranda
- Prosecution and declination files

Material Type:

• Indictments

• Affidavits

• Prosecutorial decisions

• Correspondence between U.S. Attorneys

Location:

National Archives at Washington, D.C. (Archives I)

Some files stored at College Park (Archives II)

B. Record Group 105 — Freedmen's Bureau

Title: Bureau of Refugees, Freedmen, and Abandoned Lands

Relevant Series:

• Labor contract registers

• Complaints of abuse

• Agent correspondence

• Court case summaries

Time Period:

1865–1872

C. Record Group 29 — Census Bureau

Relevant Materials:

• Manuscript Census Schedules

• Population classification tables

• Occupational data

• Mortality schedules

D. Record Group 233 — House of Representatives

Relevant Materials:

• Congressional investigative committee records

• Civil Rights hearings

• Testimony transcripts

PART III

STATE ARCHIVES (VARIES BY CHAPTER)

A. Mississippi Department of Archives and History

Records:

- 1955 Emmett Till trial transcript
- Indictments
- Jury records
- County-level filings

B. State Department of Corrections Archives

Materials:

- Convict leasing contracts
- Prison labor assignment logs
- Medical treatment registers

C. County Coroner / Medical Examiner Offices

Records:

- Inquest transcripts
- Autopsy registers
- Cause-of-death documentation

PART IV

MEDICAL & INSTITUTIONAL ARCHIVES

National Library of Medicine (Bethesda, MD)

Collections:

- Institutional research records
- Public health program documentation
- Historical hospital administrative papers

State Hospital Archives

Materials:

- Institutional admission records
- Medical experimentation documentation
- Oversight reports

Access varies by state.

PART V

FEDERAL STATUTES & LEGISLATIVE RECORDS

United States Statutes at Large

Location:

Law libraries; Library of Congress; Government Publishing Office

Use to verify:

• Reconstruction Acts

• Civil Rights Acts

• Voting Rights Act (1965)

Congressional Record

Location:

Library of Congress

Government Printing Office archives

Use to verify:

• Floor debates

• Legislative intent

• Committee reports

PART VI

STATISTICAL & POLICY DATA

Bureau of Labor Statistics (Historical Series)

Contains:

• Wage studies

• Labor participation data

• Occupational disparity reports

Statistical Abstract of the United States (1878–2012)

Contains:

• Population breakdowns

• Economic disparity tables

• Mortality and incarceration data

RESEARCH RETRIEVAL INSTRUCTIONS FOR READERS

When visiting archives:

1. Register as a researcher
2. Identify Record Group (RG) or Series
3. Note date range
4. Request box or file by catalog number
5. Photograph or request digital reproduction

Most institutions require advance file request submission.

COUNTER-ARGUMENT & CRITICAL RESPONSE

Addressing Methodological, Historical, and Interpretive Challenges

I. "These events are exaggerated."

Response:

This work relies on primary documentation produced contemporaneously by courts, legislatures, commercial entities, and administrative institutions. Claims are not based on folklore, rumor, or retrospective storytelling.

Where interpretation occurs, it is clearly distinguished from documented fact.

Verification is possible through:

• National archives
• Court records
• Legislative volumes
• Institutional archives

Exaggeration requires fabrication. Fabrication requires absence of documentation. The documentation exists.

II. "These were isolated incidents, not systemic patterns."

Response:

The argument of systemic pattern is not derived from singular events, but from repeated documentary structures across:

• multiple states
• multiple decades

- multiple institutions
- multiple categories of record

When legal statutes, administrative practices, and statistical outcomes align over long periods, historians classify the phenomenon as structural, not incidental.

III. "Historical actors were operating within the norms of their time."

Response:

The presence of opposition during the same historical period undermines this defense. Contemporary dissent, abolition movements, civil rights challenges, and legal protests demonstrate that alternatives existed.

Documentation of debate within legislative records confirms that policies were choices, not inevitabilities.

IV. "Records are incomplete — conclusions may be speculative."

Response:

Archival loss is acknowledged. Where records are incomplete, conclusions are limited to what is supported.

No claim in this work depends solely on missing evidence. Where silence exists in the archive, it is treated as silence, not filled with assumption.

V. "The book assigns moral judgment to historical systems."

Response:

This work presents documented events and institutional structures. Moral interpretation is secondary to documentary evidence.

When court cases, statutes, or official memoranda are quoted, they speak for themselves.

VI. "This work invites present-day blame."

Response:

The work examines historical systems and documented decisions. It does not assign guilt to living individuals. It focuses on institutions and documented policy structures.

VII. "Comparisons to modern scandals are rhetorical."

Response:

Structural comparisons are used analytically, not emotionally. Similarities are examined in terms of:

- power dynamics
- legal framing
- prosecutorial decisions
- administrative discretion

The comparison concerns institutional behavior patterns, not equivalency of context.

HISTORIOGRAPHICAL POSITIONING

This work aligns with documentary-based historical analysis used in:

- legal history
- economic history
- institutional history
- archival studies

It does not rely on:

- anonymous testimony
- unverified rumor
- secondary speculation without primary backing

EVIDENCE TRANSPARENCY STATEMENT

Readers are provided with:

- archival record group numbers
- case names
- repository locations
- citation formats

This level of transparency allows independent verification.

INTERPRETIVE LIMITATION CLAUSE

Where interpretation extends beyond documentation, it is identified as interpretation. Where documentation is silent, silence is preserved.

INTERNATIONAL, MARITIME, AND HUMAN RIGHTS FRAMEWORKS

Legal Violations, Structural Legacy, and the Question of Remedy

The historical systems documented in this book, including maritime trafficking, coerced labor regimes, sexual exploitation, extrajudicial violence, and medical abuse, would violate multiple contemporary bodies of law if evaluated under present standards.

The fact that many of these events predate modern codifications does not erase their incompatibility with today's legal principles.

The following frameworks are relevant.

I. MARITIME LAW & UNCLOS

United Nations Convention on the Law of the Sea (UNCLOS)

UNCLOS establishes obligations concerning:

suppression of piracy (Art. 100–107)

prohibition of slave transport (customary maritime law recognition)

duty to rescue persons in distress at sea (Art. 98)

Although UNCLOS (1982) postdates the transatlantic system, the prohibition against slavery and slave transport was already recognized as customary international law by the 19th century and codified in earlier conventions such as:

1815 Congress of Vienna Declaration

1890 Brussels Act

1926 Slavery Convention

The forced maritime transport of human beings as cargo would violate:

Freedom of navigation principles

Prohibitions against trafficking

Duties of humane treatment at sea

Today, such conduct would also constitute:

Crimes against humanity under international criminal law

Human trafficking under the Palermo Protocol

II. INTERNATIONAL HUMAN RIGHTS LAW

The documented practices described in this book would violate core provisions of:

Universal Declaration of Human Rights (1948)

Article 1: All human beings are born free and equal in dignity and rights

Article 4: No one shall be held in slavery or servitude

Article 5: No one shall be subjected to torture or cruel, inhuman or degrading treatment

Article 7: Equal protection of the law

International Covenant on Civil and Political Rights (ICCPR)

Article 7: Prohibition of torture

Article 8: Prohibition of slavery and forced labor

Article 9: Protection against arbitrary detention

Article 26: Equal protection without discrimination

International Convention on the Elimination of All Forms of Racial Discrimination (ICERD)

Prohibits racial discrimination in legal, political, economic, and social structures

Requires states to eliminate structural racial hierarchies

The racialized systems described in historical records directly conflict with these principles.

III. CRIMES AGAINST HUMANITY FRAMEWORK

Under the Rome Statute of the International Criminal Court (ICC):

Crimes against humanity include:

Enslavement

Deportation or forcible transfer

Rape and sexual violence

Persecution against identifiable groups

Other inhumane acts intentionally causing great suffering

The transatlantic system and many successor structures would fall within these definitions if evaluated under modern standards.

IV. DOMESTIC U.S. LAW

While earlier eras legally sanctioned certain practices, modern U.S. constitutional doctrine recognizes protections including:

13th Amendment (Abolition of Slavery)

14th Amendment (Equal Protection Clause)

15th Amendment (Voting Rights)

Civil Rights Act (1964)

Voting Rights Act (1965)

42 U.S.C. § 1983 (Civil Rights Enforcement)

Many of the systems examined in this book are inconsistent with modern constitutional protections.

V. STRUCTURAL LEGACY & PRESENT CONDITIONS

A critical legal question is not whether current law permits historical abuses, it does not, but whether the structural consequences of those systems remain measurable.

Scholars examine continuity through:

Wealth gaps

Land dispossession records

Housing discrimination redlining archives

Incarceration statistics

Health disparities

Educational access inequities

The legal significance lies in whether past state-sanctioned systems created durable disadvantages traceable through documentation.

Courts evaluating reparative claims often examine:

Historical causation

Government participation

Ongoing disparate impact

Statutes of limitation

Sovereign immunity

Standing requirements

The existence of documentation strengthens claims of historical causation, though legal remedies face procedural barriers.

VI. RIGHT TO REMEDY UNDER INTERNATIONAL LAW

International human rights doctrine recognizes:

The Right to an Effective Remedy

Articulated in:

UDHR Article 8

ICCPR Article 2(3)

UN Basic Principles on the Right to a Remedy and Reparation (2005)

Remedies may include:

Restitution

Compensation

Rehabilitation

Satisfaction (truth commissions, public acknowledgment)

Guarantees of non-repetition

The debate surrounding reparations for transatlantic slavery and racialized legal systems centers on whether:

The harm constitutes a continuing violation

The state remains legally responsible

Remedies are enforceable in domestic courts

This remains an evolving area of legal scholarship.

VII. LEGAL CAUTION & CLARITY

It is important to state clearly:

Modern Afrodescendant Americans are not legally classified under the frameworks that governed historical systems of enslavement.

However, legal scholars debate whether:

Documented historical state action created enduring structural effects that may give rise to claims grounded in equal protection, unjust enrichment, international law principles, or transitional justice models.

That debate is ongoing.

CONCLUSION

The systems documented in this book would violate:

Maritime law norms

Human trafficking prohibitions

Anti-slavery conventions

Human rights treaties

Constitutional protections

International criminal law standards

The central legal question today is not whether those systems were lawful under their own time, many were, but whether their documented harms create obligations under contemporary principles of justice, remedy, and non-repetition.

The archive does not answer that question.

It provides the evidence upon which it must be debated.

OFFICIAL STATEMENT ON SCOPE AND CONTINUATION

Regarding the General Audience Edition

This volume is intentionally restrained.

It presents a documented historical and legal examination of systems that shaped the lives of Afrodescendant people in the Americas and across the diaspora. It draws from maritime records, court proceedings, legislative archives, institutional files, medical publications, and public reports. It identifies categories of harm and traces the administrative structures that sustained them.

However, it does not exhaust the record.

The historical archive contains material of far greater severity than what appears here. The primary sources document not only forced labor and legal exclusion, but systematic sexual violence, coerced reproduction, trafficking networks, public terror spectacles, medical exploitation, family separation regimes, psychological domination practices, and other forms of abuse recorded in the language of their time.

Many of these materials are explicit.

Many are deeply disturbing.

Many have rarely been synthesized into accessible historical analysis.

This edition omits detailed sensory reconstruction of those records for deliberate reasons:

To prevent retraumatization through gratuitous imagery

To avoid turning suffering into spectacle

To maintain analytical clarity over emotional shock

To ensure accessibility for a broader readership

The brutality documented in archival files does not require embellishment. The institutional record itself confirms its severity.

Yet it must be acknowledged plainly:

This book represents only a foundational examination.

The full historical record includes documentation of:

sexual coercion embedded within legal property systems

forced reproductive policies designed for economic expansion

organized trafficking networks operating through maritime and domestic channels

public executions and ritualized terror events

documented medical experimentation without consent

systemic family separation

institutionalized humiliation practices

economic extraction of bodily labor and identity

coordinated legal mechanisms designed to maintain racial hierarchy

transnational patterns affecting Afrodescendants beyond the United States

The archive also preserves lesser-known regional case files, probate records, insurance disputes, plantation correspondence, military orders, health board directives, and international trade documentation that have not yet been fully integrated into a comprehensive narrative.

A subsequent volume may be necessary.

Such a continuation would engage the unfiltered archival material directly. It would analyze explicit primary documents in their original language. It would confront the most difficult dimensions of the historical record with scholarly rigor and evidentiary precision.

That work requires preparation.

It requires readers prepared to encounter documentation in its raw form. It requires careful framing to prevent distortion or sensationalism. And it requires the same commitment to verification that governs this volume.

This edition lays the structural groundwork.

It establishes the legal frameworks, administrative systems, and evidentiary foundations necessary to understand the scale of what occurred.

The deeper excavation remains.

History does not become less true because it is difficult to print.

But responsible scholarship sometimes proceeds in stages.

This is the first stage.

The full archive waits.

Made in the USA
Monee, IL
05 November 2026

68030325R00121